A Room Full of Mirrors

KEIKO IKEDA

A Room
Full of Mirrors

High School Reunions in Middle America

STANFORD UNIVERSITY PRESS

STANFORD, CALIFORNIA

1998

Stanford University Press
Stanford, California

© 1998 by the Board of Trustees
of the Leland Stanford Junior University

Printed in the United States of America

CIP data appear at the end of the book

To my son, Izumi Alexis,
who may someday attend high school
in the United States

A little scene frequently comes back to me. It occurred at a reunion of the "war-years" classes of a suburban New York high school. All the festivities were over and I was moving along with a crowd of well-dressed people coming out of the hall to find their way home. Their faces glowed. Some were still frantically talking, making promises of future contact or plans to get together the next day before leaving for California, Minnesota, Colorado—those places where they led their adult lives. As I neared the exit, two women approached me hurriedly, as if they had urgent business. One woman was tall and was wearing a plain dress; the other short, wearing a white blouse, dark blue skirt, and thick glasses—modest attire in comparison to that of the other reunion participants. They asked if I had learned as much as I expected. They were aware that I was attending their reunion for the purpose of an-thropological study—I had been introduced by the Master of Cere-monies. "Coming to this reunion meant a lot to us," said the taller woman, and her friend, with a warm, shy smile, nodded in agreement. "A class reunion is like going back in history and finding out things you've never thought about before." They seemed determined to com-municate to me a deeply felt experience that I—as an outsider—might have missed in the excitement of the activities. Apologizing that they had to catch a flight home early the next morning and wishing me luck, they melted into the crowd of people waiting for cabs, leaving me with the enormous task of understanding what their words really meant.

The high school reunion is a popular event throughout the United States, cutting across locality and age. Generally considered a light-hearted social occasion that has little significance in people's lives, it is in fact a rich and often poignant experience for many Americans. Though I didn't meet those two women again, I did meet and speak at length with many Americans who shared their reunion experiences and sentiments with me.

Why are high school reunions a compelling experience for many Americans? I examine this popular ritual as a dramatic event in the construction of self and meaning in American adulthood. I argue that the high school reunion provides adult Americans with an opportunity to evaluate and examine their unfolding biographies. Moreover, in the reflexive processes that emerge in the reunion, participants construct new stories and symbols. These, in turn, give direction to individual sense-making activities in a way that reflects both culture and history.

In Chapter 1, I discuss my perspective as an ethnographer. Unlike most ethnographies, which are accounts of another culture written for an audience that more or less shares the author's cultural background, mine is a Japanese interpretation of American experience written for an American audience. I discuss the pathway this Japanese ethnographer followed in coming to terms with phenomena that most Americans take for granted.

In Chapter 2, I discuss the theoretical background of the notions of self, lifecourse, and reflexivity that I draw on throughout my ethnography, and analyze the ways in which the reunion fosters reflexivity and creates meaning.

In Chapters 3 through 5, I present examples of high school reunions and individual stories. In Chapter 3, I follow a tenth-year reunion from initial preparation to consummation, in order to demonstrate the concrete ways in which collective meaning is constructed. In Chapter 4, I show how a reunion intersects with individual biographies and how people make use of ritual occasions to achieve their own biographical goals, examining not only what ritual does to people, but what people do with ritual events. In Chapter 5, I describe a fortieth-year reunion in order to show how earlier and later reunions of a single class differ in significance for different historical cohorts, and I discuss the changeful, emergent ordering of ritual performances through time.

Finally, in Chapter 6, I try to pinpoint the unique significance of high school reunions in American adulthood by examining the socio-cultural milieu that nurtures reunions in American society.

This book would not have been possible without the help of many people. They all have my heartfelt thanks, but here I can only hope to name and thank a few, whose help and guidance formed the final shape of this book in significant ways.

I would like to thank my two mentors at the University of Illinois: Edward Bruner, an inspiring teacher with a talent for sorting out from a student's projects that which is anthropologically exciting; and David Plath, who not only introduced me to the world of anthropology, but taught me how to be intellectually tough without being dogmatic.

I also thank Clark Cunningham, Alma Gottlieb, Christie Kiefer, Janet and Charles Keller, John Stewart, Claire Farrer, Veronica Kann, Mary Weismantel, John Isaacson, and Kathleen Fine for their valuable comments and support at various stages of this project. Comments and criticisms offered by my students and colleagues at Hamilton College and at Barnard College, Columbia University, where I taught in 1990–91 and 1991–97, respectively, were a great help when I was revising my dissertation for publication. My heartfelt thanks go to the late Barbara Miller, who never lost faith in me or my project. Special thanks also go to Lucy Whalley, who did much of the transcribing, provided editorial assistance, and offered immeasurable friendship. The superb guidance of Muriel Bell at Stanford University Press made the publication of this book possible.

Matthew Thorn, my husband, provided both technical and editorial assistance in the preparation of the final draft. Critical comments he made throughout the process of writing were indispensable in shaping the interpretation I offer. My gratitude also goes to my parents in Japan, Shiro and Hisae Ikeda, for their unfaltering support from afar.

Most of all, I thank all the American people who allowed me to participate in their class reunions and shared with me their valuable experiences. Without their cooperation, this book would never have taken form outside my imagination.

The fieldwork portion of this work was supported by the Wenner-Gren Foundation for Anthropological Research and the University of Illinois Graduate College. I thank them for their generous support.

CONTENTS

A Room Full of Mirrors

1 From a Japanese Point of View

One of the weird things about going to Europe is that you start
talking about high school type things and it doesn't mean anything.
How can you describe a paper pom-pom and its manufacture—or
its sexual significance—to somebody in Vienna?

—*Frank Zappa, 1968 interview*

An ethnography is the product of a unique reflexive relationship between the ethnographer, the people she studies, and the audience to
whom she addresses her findings. An understanding of the ethnographer's point of view—personal, cultural, and anthropological—and her
position in the ethnographic universe she portrays is essential to the
evaluation of facts and interpretations.

In my study of high school reunions, this issue is doubly important
because my ethnography is the product of a peculiar interpretive di-
alogue. Unlike most ethnographic texts, mine is written for members of
the cultural community that is the subject of my ethnographic inquiry.
It therefore requires a sort of double translation: the first, to make
things "fit" into my own Japanese cultural baggage, and the second, to
make them fit back into that which my American reader carries.

In this chapter, I discuss the ethnographer's point of view. The first
section invites the American reader to travel with me along my pathway
to understanding, the intellectual and affective modes of understanding that this Japanese anthropologist drew on in coming to terms with
one of the most taken-for-granted phenomena in American society. At
the same time, the chapter will allow the American reader to peek into

my own "cultural baggage," and possibly to comprehend the "Japanese perspective" at work throughout my ethnography. In the second section, I discuss my methodological perspective as a cultural interpreter.

High School in Two Cultures

"So, you are studying high school reunions and you want to interview me," said the woman on the phone. She is sixty-eight years old, a lifelong resident of Champaign-Urbana, and was organizing a fiftieth-year reunion for her graduating class of 1932. I found her telephone number in a newspaper advertisement asking for information about her Elm High classmates whom she could not locate. Her voice was gentle and friendly but had an inquisitive and skeptical tone.

"What field are you in? Psychology?"

"No, anthropology."

"Oh, I thought that anthropologists dig old bones and . . ."

"Well, I'm a cultural anthropologist. I study living people and living culture."

"Did you say you're from Japan? That's interesting. You came all the way from Japan to study high school reunions! I've never heard of anybody in a university who studies this kind of thing." She paused for a short while and asked, "Does your professor approve of that for your dissertation?"

One of the things that intrigued me during the course of my research was the way that people reacted when they first encountered a Japanese anthropologist whose aim was to study high school reunions in the United States. Their reactions ranged from amusement to fascination. For most of the Americans with whom I spoke, the class reunion is such a commonplace event that they had never thought of it as being a subject of serious academic interest. For example, two papers on high school reunions appeared in the same issue of the *Journal of Popular Culture* in 1985. Each gives a description of the author's own reunion experiences, but little interpretive insight.[1] Although the poignant nature of reunions in adulthood is sometimes noted, there has not been any systematic or intensive study relating lifecourse to the significance of the reunion in human development.[2]

Seen from a Japanese perspective, however, the high school reunion is a fascinating cultural event. Although the phenomenon of reunions associated with all levels of educational experience is not an alien concept in Japanese society, the main features of reunions (to be discussed in Chapter 2) are not as prevalent or uniform as in the United States.[3]

The class reunion in America is a common topic in popular books and articles, movies, television programs, and periodicals.[4] It occurs in all towns, large and small, and in various adult age groups throughout the United States, and the organization of this social gathering is strikingly uniform and stylized. There is a general expectation shared by everyone; as one of my informants put it, "The reunion is something that we all expect to happen in our adult life." The high school reunion is rooted in popular American consciousness.

Moreover, I was struck by "the passionate interest," as Michelle Rosaldo (1980) calls it, that adult Americans demonstrate when sharing high school experiences or relating reunion stories. It seems that the subjects of high school and reunions strike Americans at their experiential core, hidden beneath the surface of present selves, provoking thoughts, sentiments, and memories. When conversation developed to the point at which exchanges of "you-know-what-I-mean" dominated, I felt alienated from the interexperiential bonding of my American friends.

At the time I started my research, I had been a resident of Champaign-Urbana, which was the main site of my field study, for nearly six years. Champaign-Urbana had become my most intimate environment—the base from which I made homecoming trips to Japan and to which I "came back" to lead my "normal" routine. My experience in America had become one of the most significant parts of my own biography, and my ethnographic Others had become my "convoy," to use Plath's phrase (1980), the people without whom my biography cannot be written. The alienation I felt when faced with American discourse on high school, however, reminded me of my foreignness—a foreignness that sprang from the fact that I did not share a significant portion of my cultural biography with my American friends. I therefore came to realize that even if I share the present life world of my American friends, I do not share with them the memories and sentiments shaped by their cultural experience—in their past and in my absence.

As my fascination with American discourse on high school reunions grew, I rediscovered the ethnographic Other in my American friends.

"I wonder why we make such a big deal about high school reunions in our society. Do you have reunions in Japan? Are they different from ours?" asked an insurance company executive when I told him that I was studying high school reunions in America.

"Yes we do, but—"

"It seems to me," he continued, "that reunions must be a really American thing—like the Superbowl or something."

The setting for this conversation was a party being held by a middle-aged professor and his fiancée at their suburban Champaign-Urbana home on the night before their wedding. They had invited both friends and relatives, and, though the party was very middle-class, many different ages and occupations were represented.

While I was talking with this man, his wife suddenly turned away from a conversation with a friend and interjected, "My class held its twentieth-year reunion this summer, but I didn't go. I thought I had outgrown that high school mentality, you know? But now I think I'd like to go to the next one, because I feel like I missed something."

"Oh, you should go," her friend joined in. "At my twentieth it was really interesting to see that so many people who were considered to be successful in high school turned out to be local small-time businessmen, and a lot of those kids who nobody ate lunch with, you know, turned out to be doctors and lawyers."

The conversation rippled out toward a wider circle. A graphic designer in her late thirties who had gone to high school in Boulder, Colorado, said, "Yeah, there was this girl in my class, she was a cheerleader and queen and everything, you know? She came to our fifteenth-year reunion. She was married and had three kids, and all she did at the reunion was show everyone pictures of her kids! Boy, she looked as old as everybody else!" (laugh).

"I hated those stuck-ups," a man in his early forties who is an active member of a local tennis club responded, "I have no desire to go back and see them."

Then the tennis player's wife chimed in: "My mother just got an invitation to her fiftieth-year reunion. She is so excited about going back to her hometown in Ohio. It's funny to see the way she is now. The other day she called to ask me to come over and help her decide what to wear to the reunion. When I got there she had her whole wardrobe laid out on the bed and said, 'Janet, how about this dress? Does it make me look old? How about this one? No, it makes me look fat . . .' (laugh). I felt like a mother sending her daughter off to the senior prom!"

Most Americans can understand and intimately relate to this conversation, even though they may have gone to different high schools in different parts of the country. But what was difficult to grasp from the point of view of a Japanese anthropologist, whose cultural biography does not include an American high school, was the affective meaning particular high school idioms carry, and the memories and sentiments associated with it.

What do they mean by "that high school mentality"? Why is it intriguing to find that "the ones nobody ate lunch with" became doctors and lawyers? Or what is funny about a woman who used to be "a cheerleader and queen and everything" turning out to be a happy mother, "looking as old as anybody else"? What kind of sentiments was the tennis player communicating when he said that he "hated those stuck-ups"? How *should* you feel the night before a "prom"? Isn't it just another school activity? Of course, I understood the meaning intellectually, but not to the point of feeling, as most Americans do, the experiential texture and affective orientation hidden in the "you-knows" of high school symbols and discourse.

How, then, would I overcome the biographical distance between myself and my Others? How would I achieve a "fusion of horizon" (Gadamer 1982), to enter the experiential world of my informants and to make that world—at least partially—my own?

If I were conducting a field study of high school itself, there would be a concrete community where I could locate myself to participate and observe enough, possibly, to come to "feel how they feel." But the community I am studying is a community of memory.[5] This community was formed long ago, in high school, and re-forms periodically in adult years in the context of reunions. No new name can be added to its membership list.

In order to overcome this biographical gap on my part, and to make the American reader understand why this Japanese observer feels perplexed and fascinated by the peculiar affective weight given to things related to high school, we must turn our attention for a moment to what seem to me the unique features of American high school and the ways in which high school symbols are used in cultural discourse.

The American high school has evolved from the Latin grammar school of the seventeenth century and the academies of the eighteenth century. America's first high school appeared in Boston in 1821. But the institution as we know it today was not established until the end of the nineteenth century. In 1870, there were only 160 high schools in the nation. By 1890, the number had jumped to 6,005. Since that time, high schools have spread across the nation, and by the time the oldest high school class I studied graduated (Elm High School Class of 1932), the number of high schools in America was 22,237. The national census shows a correspondingly dramatic increase in high school enrollment. In 1890, only 6.7 percent of fourteen- to seventeen-year-olds were enrolled in public or private high schools. This figure increased sharply over the following decades, reaching 51.4 percent in 1930. By 1950, enrollment was almost 80 percent, and the numbers continued to increase steadily until in 1972 (the year the youngest high school class that I had studied graduated), 93.5 percent of adolescent boys and girls in America were entering high school, with about 76 percent graduating.[6]

Japanese secondary education shows a similar pattern of growth. As in the United States, secondary education began to appear in Japan at the end of the nineteenth century. In 1895, only 1.1 percent of high-school age children were enrolled. By 1915, enrollment had increased to 19.9 percent, and then doubled in the next twenty years (to 39.7 percent). Following the educational reforms brought about by the American Occupation, this figure jumped to 61.7 percent in 1947. High school attendance increased rapidly thereafter, and by 1978, 96.2 percent of adolescent boys and girls were enrolled in high schools.[7] The percentage of students graduating is higher (about 96 percent) in Japan than in the United States.[8] Today, high school education is firmly entrenched in the social systems of both countries.

The sociological impetus behind the universal development of high schools in both nations is associated with historical trends they experienced in the twentieth century. Industrialization and the expansion of the middle class, in particular, fostered the ideology of providing an equal education for all. In Japan, for example, the development of secondary education was the result of the nation's efforts to create an egalitarian school system. The Meiji Restoration of 1868 led to the replacement of the traditional system by one based on European models, one that would educate "citizens" as befit an industrial Japan. The joint efforts of the Japanese and the American Occupation government after World War II drastically reformed Japanese schools, creating a system intended to educate "individuals" appropriate to a democratic Japan.[9] Similarly, in the United States, the development of the comprehensive high school, which James B. Conant called a "unique American institution," is considered to be intimately tied to the pursuit of democratic ideals.[10] In theory if not in practice, the American high school aims at providing an equal education to all future citizens of the nation.

Even though postwar Japanese secondary education was modeled on the American system, Japanese high schools differ significantly on two points.[11] First, in spite of the efforts of the Occupation, the "comprehensive secondary school" did not become dominant in Japan. Today, only one-third of high schools have comprehensive programs, while half are exclusively academic and the remainder are exclusively vocational. A quarter of high schools in Japan are privately owned and operated, while in America most high schools are public, and private school enrollments have long been minor, serving primarily the Catholic middle class of eastern and midwestern cities. In addition, whereas all American public schools are coeducational, 10 percent of public schools and 63 percent of private schools in Japan are not.[12]

Second, compulsory education in Japan ends at the level of *chūgaku*, or middle school (seventh through ninth grades). And *kōkō*, or high school, though now attended by almost all children of eligible age, is neither compulsory nor free of charge. Whereas American high schools are open to all teenaged boys and girls of a community or attendance area and offer a broad program of academic, practical, prevocational, and vocational education, Japanese students have to choose a high school appropriate to their academic abilities and future aspirations, and they must take entrance examinations to be admitted.

In Japan, there are many schools to choose from (or to strive to enter), each with a unique character and academic ranking, defined by a school's capacity to produce graduates who can pass the entrance examinations of the better universities and colleges. Thomas Rohlen, an American anthropologist who studied four different types of high school in Japan, observed:

> Although the attention of Western scholars has focused primarily on the problem of college entrance in Japan . . . , the time of high school entrance represents an even more crucial juncture in the total process of educational stratification. Virtually the entire youth population is involved, and the educational tracks into which students are shunted at this stage are both more diverse and more fundamental than at the college stage to the overall structure of the society. The ranking of high schools in a given locality is as clear—if not clearer—to all citizens as is the ranking of universities on a national scale. At the local level, which high school a person attends carries lifetime significance, and the finely etched stereotypes of student character associated with each high school become an indelible part of individual identity. (1983: 121)

Thus, for Japanese youth, the transition from chūgaku to kōkō is not automatic, and the high school one enters critically determines one's present status and identity, and, to a large degree, one's future career path. High schools become placement offices, sorting students into educational and, eventually, social hierarchies. A natural consequence of this system is relative homogeneity in the student population of a single school; one goes to school with people of more or less the same background and ability.[13] The uniforms worn in most schools become symbols, indicating that one belongs to a particular school, and giving one an overall sense of identity and an awareness of where one stands in relation to those from other schools.

In such a system, the emphasis is on study, as students strive to gain admission to the better universities or prepare themselves for desirable careers. Although clubs are popular in Japanese high schools (and colleges and middle schools as well), many students withdraw from these extracurricular activities as the university entrance examination approaches. In this sense, high school students in Japan are already involved in "real-life" competition.

Japanese high school students, as Rohlen noted, do treasure individual friendships, follow distinct fads and fashions, and yearn for peer contacts, but the "independent group activities (parties, going out together, hanging around) and status ranking (created by cliques, dating, invitations, fraternities, sports, elections), which are at the heart of the American teen subculture, are of little consequence."[14] It is exactly this emphasis on student activities separate from the formal classroom setting and on the social life of students that stands out as unique to the comprehensive American high school from a Japanese perspective.

In sharp contrast to its Japanese counterpart, the ideal public high school in the United States should bring together boys and girls of different social classes, academic abilities, and personal talents. A miniature society is generated that in principle duplicates the social stratification of the community. Since attendance areas are predefined, American youth always have a high school to go to, or, to put it differently, "the situation has been one of little consumer choice" for most students (Coleman et al. 1974: 79). Schools are deeply grounded in the community, and it is often the case that students go to school with the same children they grew up with, particularly in smaller towns.

The perception of the function of high school is very different from that in Japan, as well. High school in America is commonly thought of as a period of "moratorium which postpones for a few more years the eventual assignment of students to educational tracks that lead to different careers and life chances" (ibid., 74).

As early as 1924, Lynd and Lynd described this "moratorium" as they saw it in Middletown:

> Accompanying the formal training afforded by the courses of study is another and informal kind of training, particularly during the high school years. The high school, with its athletics, clubs, sororities and fraternities, dances and parties, and other "extracurricular activities," is a fairly complete social cosmos in itself, and about this city within a city the social life of the intermediate generation centers. Here the social sifting devices of their elders—money, clothes, personal attractiveness, male physical prowess, exclusive

clubs, election to positions of leadership—are all for the first time set going with a population as yet largely undifferentiated save as regards their business class and working class parents. This informal training is not a preparation for a vague future that must be taken on trust, as is the case with so much of the academic work; to many boys and girls in high school this is "the life," the thing they personally like best about going to school. (1956: 211)

Even though they are under the autonomous control of such communities as Middletown, public high schools across the nation and across time are similar in social structure and school activities. I was impressed, during the course of my research, by the ubiquity and timelessness of certain high school events and personality types that appeared again and again in the stories recounted by my informants of various ages and of different local origins. When asked about their most memorable high school experiences, my informants told stories of ball games, proms, clubs, student government, interpersonal relationships, conflicts between cliques, feelings of rejection, struggles to gain acceptance from peers, dating, and unrequited love.

Many studies, each conducted at a different time and locality, similarly point out that high schools in America form a characteristic "microcosm" with a distinctive social and value system and an elaborated ceremonial calendar.[15] Gordon (1957) found that the informal social life of high school peers—one of the subsystems he identified in a suburban high school in a midwestern metropolitan community—comprises a powerful agent that controls and influences adolescent behavior.

Whereas in Japan, as Rohlen noted, high school students are defined as "children" both by adults and by the students themselves, and the transition from childhood to adulthood (as in many other non-Western societies) is not dominated by status or identity ambiguity, adolescence in the United States is commonly considered to be a period of struggle for identity—the stage between childhood and adulthood in which teenagers struggle to overcome existential ambiguities associated with this liminal phase. The microcosm created in the context of secondary education constitutes a powerful "behavioral environment," to use Hallowell's (1967) phrase, in which high school students struggle to complete this developmental task—to grasp a consistent, gratifying self-image, a vision for adulthood, and to establish an adult identity. And high school events, activities, and personality types form parts of the symbolic system within which adolescent boys and girls confront these developmental tasks.

The symbolic system of high school works to define status-ranking and the self-images of high school students.[16] The whole annual round of high school life is marked by rituals for status evaluation that propagate the desired images of American personhood (proms, ball games, elections, cheerleader tryouts, popularity contests, etc.). Such images include, for example, what can be called authorized ideals of "maleness" (athlete, class leader) and "femaleness" (prom queen, cheerleader).

Students develop a definitive terminology (symbols) for classifying dominant personality types and recurrent personality traits (cheerleader, jock, class brain, bookworm, wallflower, class clown, loner, jerk, stuck-up, etc.). Peer groups known as cliques develop within the high school environment. The distinctive styles of speech, behavior, and dress adopted by members of cliques serve as signs for assigning an individual student to a particular category and group. Consequently, membership in a particular clique becomes itself an identity symbol that defines an individual's place in the status system of high school.

One of my informants, Cindy, describes her struggle to fit into one such category:

> I wanted to be a cheerleader real bad and I knew I'd never get
> elected if I wasn't popular. So every year of my life in school I always
> made a New Year's resolution: "This year I'm not going to say shitty
> things to people. I'm going to be nice, I'm going to be popular."
> And I knew all the things a person had to be to be popular. You had
> to be sweet. You had to be funny. You had to dress nice. You had to
> be a candidate for a lot of things, and to be asked out. And, as a
> woman, you had to be a little stupid, to act kind of dumb. So I always had a double life, because I was smart and I made good grades.
>
> From my sophomore year, I started to get nominated for things.
> I was track queen, I was sportsmanship queen, and in my senior
> year I was actually elected by the student body to be cheerleader
> and was up for Homecoming Queen. I was one of the four finalists.

So by my senior year I realized, "Oh, I'm popular, because I've gotten up for these things." But then I thought, "Well, but I'm still not asked out on very many dates."

The behavioral and symbolic environment of high school is a testing ground for personhood and for potential as a legitimate adult in American society. As many of my informants emphasized, the daily struggle of acting in and against this symbolic environment creates a lot of social pressure. And for many it is traumatic. Cindy is very explicit about the peer pressure she felt in school.

In high school, the opinion of other people just mattered too much. That was the most painful thing. Just every day. It was grinding, you know. Kids are mean. They're vicious. And they'll do anything to bring you down to size. It's really frightening at the time. Down to where if you wear certain colors on certain days, or whatever, those all have connotations that you just torture people with. If you walk through the middle door on Thursday it means you're queer. Nobody even knew what that meant, to be queer.

High school may be the first, and perhaps also the last, time in one's life that is spent with a social and economic cross-section of peers, exposed to the comprehensive and merciless judgment of others. Keyes (1976: 34) writes, recalling his own high school experience, "Never again are we ranked so precisely by those around us, and on so many scales. Through the popularity polls of our classmates, and their inexperience at tact, daily feedback was conveyed about how we were coming across. Such merciless judgment is not easily forgotten, the last time of life we know just where we stand in the scrutinizing eyes around us."

Cultural differences in the high school experiences of Americans and Japanese spring from the different emphases the two societies place on high school education. High school students in contemporary Japan are separated from adult responsibilities in the confinement of school, devoting themselves to struggling through "examination hell" in order to obtain authentic passage to adulthood and to learn the realities of the Japanese social hierarchy. Today, with the dramatic expansion of the middle class, the pressure to "get ahead" is enormous. The Japanese media refer to the phenomenon of *juken jigoku* ("examination hell"), which sometimes starts as early as elementary school, as "a national rite" in postwar Japan.[17]

American students, by contrast, though enjoying a "moratorium" in terms of eventual career assignment, have to endure the hell of the critical gaze, so to speak, of their peers, and face continual evaluation in a system of symbols and status-ranking within which they must win popularity, friendship, romance, and eventually a sense of self on which they can build their future. In an American society in miniature, they learn the rhetoric of their culture and are introduced to the larger society's vision(s) of ideal personhood.

It is frequently pointed out that American high school students are conformists or other-oriented. Since adolescence in America is framed in structural ambiguity, constant identification with others and affirmation from them, especially one's classmates, are important for a healthy transition through this stage of life. As Erikson (1950) points out, there is always a potential danger of role confusion. Because of the traumatic and future-oriented character of the teenager's search for self in the school setting, many scholars and lay observers see the institutionalized confinement of adolescents in high school as a rite of passage unique to industrialized America.

"Human life is a continuous thread which each of us spins to his own patterns, rich and complex in meaning. There are no natural knots in it. Yet knots form, nearly always in adolescence," says Edgar Friedenberg in *Coming of Age in America* (1963: 3). Adolescent years are important for the development of self both in the United States and in Japan. Yet different institutional emphases in secondary education foster different experiential meanings and biographical significances. Given the comprehensive and inclusive character of high school experience that I have just described, high school in America constitutes a far more powerful common denominator for cultural biography than in Japan and naturally shapes unique cultural memories and sentiments associated with this institutional experience. And the symbol system born in the educational setting is carried beyond the immediate context and included in "the cultural symbols that identify experience" (Plath 1980: 3).

In Japanese cultural discourse, for example, educational idioms are often used outside the school context, but these idioms are not derived strictly from high school, but from the entirety of educational competition. For example, the popular slogan *yon-tō, go-raku*, or "four hours pass, five hours fail," is an expression used by students preparing for entrance examinations that invokes the presumed relationship between the amount of time a student sleeps each night and success or failure on the examination. But adults use this phrase too, saying, for example, "We have to overcome this hardship with the spirit of *yon-tō, go-raku*." Personality types, such as *yūtōsei* ("honor student") and *rettōsei* ("inferior student") are commonly used to label adult characters (e.g., "He is a snobbish *yūtōsei* type"). Here again these are not just high school types but can be found at any stage of education, from elementary school to university. Perhaps because of the diversity of high schools, the lack of a uniform symbolic system in Japanese high schools, and a cultural perception of high school as one step in the educational ladder, the total process of academic competition—and not high school per se—generates cultural symbols.

In contrast, American high school symbols, such as distinctive personality types or typical events or episodes, extend their semantic efficacy beyond the immediate context of high school and pervade the cultural discourse. In what follows, I will explore how these symbols are used (or what they do), and how they are assembled to create cultural scenarios for life after high school in American discourse.

Cultural Discourse on High School

Every now and then in the United States we hear people compare life with high school. When I was watching television coverage of the 1984 presidential debate with a friend in California, he commented cynically that the presidential election seemed like nothing more than the election of a high school class president. Explaining her feelings the night before her fifteenth-year reunion, a divorcée with three children said that it was just like the night before her senior prom. An American anthropologist, Michelle Rosaldo, recalled the "hoods" from her high school days when she encountered and tried to make sense of the songs of the agitated Ilongot youths of the Philippines, who sang of their hopes to marry and to kill as part of the ritual of headhunting (1980: 337). In the cultural discourse of the United States, especially in the mass media, high school symbols and metaphors appear again and again when adults try to make sense of incidents in their own and others' lives, or when they try to render "unknown" others into "known" types.

The power of American high school symbols lies in their capacity to act as cultural symbols by linking individual memories of high school, which consist of recollections of interactions with specific friends and foes in a particular time and place. The symbols are rich with experiential and affective meanings, but as culturally specific meanings they are widely understood and are taken for granted by most Americans. Perhaps it is because, as Kurt Vonnegut Jr. claimed (1970: 60):

> High school is closer to the core of American experience than anything else I can think of . . . We have all been there. While there we saw nearly every form of justice and injustice, kindness and meanness, intelligence and stupidity, which we were likely to encounter in later life. Richard Nixon is a familiar type from high school. So is Melvin Laird. So is J. Edgar Hoover. So is General Lewis Hershey. So is everybody.

Or, as Ralph Keyes noted, high school may be "the most tribal experience [an American] will ever have." "Somehow years, even decades after graduation, no categories for making sense of the world seem to improve on the ones we learned in high school." He continues:

> "She's still queen of the hop," we say, or "a real cheerleader type." A vulgarian to Americans is one who uses "locker-room language." Then there's that completely untranslatable concept, "high school mentality." "He's got a high school mentality, know what I mean?" Of course I know. I went to high school. And since most of us have, using such terms makes it likely we'll be understood from Boston to Burbank. (1976: 37)

High school symbols, when used in adult discourse, are effective because they are taken from an intimate semantic and experiential domain (i.e., high school) shared by many Americans. High school metaphors are unique in their ability to relate two temporal, experiential dimensions—the present and one's high school years. In metaphorical movement (Burke 1945), Americans see high school from the vantage point of adulthood, and adulthood from the vantage point of high school. For example, the popular newspaper columnist Erma Bombeck characterized her return to her alma mater to receive an honorary doctorate as being similar to a cheerleader tryout. She writes:

> As I stood up to make my acceptance speech, it all came back. Cheerleader tryout. Margie Krescher wearing a turtleneck sweater that hung LOOSE around her neck. Holly Harper, who didn't have room in her arms for bones. Suzie Werle, who hadn't cut her hair since the third grade (and it was sapping all the strength away from her brain). I knew every single word of the cheers. Every movement was flawless. I jumped like I had springs in my feet. I was the only one who did the entire routine carrying a handbag. As I looked over the crowd of well-wishers, I clutched the leather-bound honorary degree and blurted out, "Don't try to make up now. It's too late! Where were you when I had fat thighs and a cheerleader wish?"[18]

Let us now focus our attention on what I call typification symbols—the symbols that act as vehicles for organizing projected images and typing adult personalities. The typification is abstracted from one's own repeated experiences and objectified in a unit of language, such as "cheerleader," "prom queen," "nerd," "jock," or "greaser."

One of my informants, who had spent years in Japan, after fumbling for a long time to explain to me what the word "nerd" means, commented:

> You see similar types in Japan but they aren't subsumed under a single, specifically "high school" term, as they are in America. Any American who hears the word "nerd" instantly thinks of that kid in high school with the high-water pants, the vinyl pencil holder in his shirt pocket, the tortoise shell glasses with the tape around the bridge and the elastic strap. There may not have been anyone exactly like that, but there were people who had that "essence," and everyone had a pretty clear idea of who they were. That image is an icon that sums up all nerds.

Image complexes of high school characters are condensed into symbols and work to typify people, especially those one does not know well enough, or about whom one does not have first-hand information. Bombeck, for instance, claimed in the same column that she could "walk into a roomful of people and with 90 percent accuracy point out those who have been cheerleaders. I can tell without being told that Dyan Cannon was a cheerleader. She's a laugher. Eydie Gorme was a cheerleader. She's cute. Dinah Shore was a cheerleader. She's popular. Patty Hearst was a cheerleader. She's rich. Raquel Welch was a cheerleader. She can do pyramids without anyone standing on her shoulders." She went on to say that she would bet that Alexander Haig had always wanted to be a cheerleader. So had Johnny Carson, and so had Erma Bombeck herself.

When used in character descriptions, typification symbols operate in two metaphorical directions. The first is present to past: the high school identity of a person is inferred by an assessment of images projected by that person in the present in terms of high school symbols—i.e., the commonplace cognitive exercise of matching impressions of an adult with a high school type.

One good illustration is a matching game invented by Keyes on the basis of his collection of instances in which public figures were described by the press in high school metaphors. He provided each description with a list of possible matches and invited his readers to play matching games. For instance:

> (1) On stage she sometimes projects the air of a spoiled, slightly heartless prom queen. (a. Lily Tomlin, b. Karen Carpenter, c. Moms Mabley, d. Gloria Steinem).
> (2) He is a high school quarterback. (a. O. J. Simpson, b. Omar Sharif, c. Fran Tarkenton, d. Woody Allen).
> (3) . . .[S]he has the waggish air of a Norman Rockwell cheerleader. (a. Bella Abzug, b. Chris Evert, c. Cybill Shepherd, d. Bette Midler).[19]

The other metaphorical movement goes in the opposite direction, past to present—information about what a person was like in high school brings out a new understanding or a sense of "knowing" that person in the present: "knowing what a person was like in high school can make, or seems to make, everything fall into place" (Keyes 1976: 45). This can be exemplified by numerous instances in which the media refer to the high school identities of public figures or of people who have done unusual things—such as receiving an award or attempting to assassinate the president—in an effort to understand how or why such things happen. For example, the *Newsweek* cover story on John Lennon's killer reported that David Chapman was a loner in high school who later became a "Jesus freak." The cover story presents Chapman's senior class picture, adding visual imagery to the narrative profile (Dec. 22, 1980: 34–35). The high school yearbook is a particularly powerful symbol: *Spy* magazine in 1991 published *Spy High: A Make-Believe Yearbook of the Rich and Famous*, featuring on the cover Roseanne Arnold, Jane Pauley, Donald Trump, Madonna, Woody Allen, Eddie Murphy, and Dan Quayle; *National Lampoon*, too, produced a spoof, the *National Lampoon 1964 High School Yearbook Parody*; the *Celebrity Yearbook*, by Dan Carlinsky, gathers yearbook pictures of hundreds of famous Americans and challenges readers to identify them.

In cultural discourse, these metaphoric associations serve to crystallize as high school symbols the changes and continuities in image trajectories of both famous and ordinary people. In the process, the discourse constructs cultural scenarios of what *type* of youths become what *type* of adults. In other words, stories emerge from the discourse that typify the kind of life each character should lead after high school. Further, scenarios so constructed are used, in turn, as symbols of identity transformation.

Protagonists in scenarios of personality transformation recur in cultural discourse as "late bloomers" (e.g., a rejected cheerleader or nerd who becomes a successful adult) or "fallen idols" (e.g., a prom queen who turns out to be a plain Jane, or a most-likely-to-succeed who fails to meet the expectations of his classmates). A good example of role reversal after high school is personified in the characters of Biff and his high school buddy Bernard in Arthur Miller's play *Death of a Salesman*. In high school, Biff, the son of a salesman, was a star football player and letterman who received a university scholarship for his athletic prowess. He was extremely popular, as his father recalls to his wife: "Remember how they followed him around in high school? When he smiled at one of them their faces lit up" (p. 16). But at the age of thirty-four, Biff is a career hobo who has not adopted an adult identity and is haunted by his high school glory and by the "would-be self" prescribed for him in his high school days. Bernard, on the other hand, who was studious in high school, was regarded as a hanger-on to his football-player friend, but now he has become an earnest, self-assured young lawyer.[20]

Protagonists who experience such role reversals are frequently featured in the plots of television dramas, especially situation comedies. In *Three's Company*, for example, Janet's romantic encounter with her high school hero—a star football player who had seemed beyond Janet's reach—teaches Janet a lesson about herself. While Janet, a flat-chested, high school wallflower, has grown up to be a sensible adult woman, her high school hero remains a "big dumb jock" whose character has not developed beyond adolescence. He has merely become an insensitive, egoistic womanizer. Although Janet loses her perduring high school dream, she gains a new understanding and esteem for her adult self.

In *Taxi*, the routine of a woman cabdriver (Elaine) is disturbed when she finds Mary, one of her former classmates with whom she led cheers, in the back seat of her cab. Elaine, now a divorced mother of two, compares her life with the success story told her by her ex-cheerleader classmate and is struck by her own perceived shortcomings. She remarks to her fellow taxi driver, "Seeing Mary reminded me that I once expected more from myself." In her high school yearbook, Elaine was listed as Most Likely To Succeed and Most Talented. She was also president of the biology club. Mary was her best competitor in the cheerleading squad. Elaine continues: "I just can't figure out why all those wonderful things are happening to her, and not to me. I am a nice, hardworking person, too. And the worst part of seeing Mary was that Mary felt sorry for me, and I felt ashamed of my own life. So I lied about having a great steady guy who is a college professor, trips to Europe together, and . . ."[21]

In the cultural discourse of American high schools, symbols are used not only to identify and categorize people, but also to create scenarios that typify changes and continuities in life or image trajectories. Thus, when television characters go to reunions, reunion episodes usually put more thematic emphasis on the comparison of lives than on a mere nostalgic return to the past. For example, Edith Bunker, at her twenty-fifth-year reunion, finds that the handsome, blond hero of her dreams has become an overweight, middle-aged man with a receding hairline.[22] A bellboy in the prime-time television drama *Hotel* suffers to overcome the disparity between his present occupation and his high school image as a football player when he must decide whether or not to attend his class reunion, to be held at the hotel where he works. Similarly, on receiving a reunion invitation, Mr. Carlson, of *WKRP in Cincinnati*, wonders in agony how "those high school kids" will treat him when they find out that the high school nobody has not yet grown up to be an adult somebody.

One older cinema portrayal of a reunion is the first segment of an omnibus picture, *Tales of Manhattan*, in which a pauper attends his class reunion dressed in a rented tailcoat to hide his true identity from his successful classmates. More recently, the main character in *Peggy Sue Got Married*, who has just separated from her husband, passes out on being named queen of her high school reunion and wakes up twenty years earlier in the body of her high school self. The common fantasy of reliving high school experiences armed with adult hindsight becomes a reality for her, and she is given the opportunity to reconsider whether or not to commit herself to the boy who would later be her husband. In *Superman III*, Clark Kent goes back to his Class of '65 reunion in Smallville, ostensibly to write a story for the *Daily Planet*. But the real purpose of his return is to find the object of his unrequited love from high school. On discovering that his beloved high school queen has divorced her football-player husband, who turns out to be an insular, alcoholic chauvinist, Clark Kent rekindles his romantic friendship with her. Indeed, the reunion episode in *Superman III* appears to be making a statement about Superman's cultural identity. Although Superman was born on another planet, he is an American hero who embodies the "right history of personal experience" (Plath 1980: 3), or at least shares a cultural root—high school—with the Americans he serves.

In reviewing American discourse on high school and class reunions, what is striking is the consistent point of view running through it. This point of view compares and contrasts the past and present self of a protagonist, or reviews a protagonist's life path after high school with an emphasis on continuity and change. The cathartic moment expected or sought in a story is an episode concluding in self-reflective understanding of achievement (as well as nonachievement), positive or negative change (as well as nonchange) in after-schoolhood, or revelation about one's life.

"Cathy" © 1981, Cathy Guisewite, Universal Press Syndicate

The catharsis a reunion can produce, however, is not always eagerly anticipated. As we can see in the accompanying comic strips, popular writers often underscore the power of reunion to subject the attendee once again to the hell of the critical gaze they endured in high school. The trepidation, or even fear, felt by many adults about attending their class reunions is a favorite target of satirists. And yet the regular appearance in the popular press of self-help articles and essays—even books—intended to help Americans prepare physically and mentally for their high school reunions would seem to indicate that many adults see it as more than just a joking matter.

Examples are too numerous to list, but one good example is a May 1985 *Family Circle* article titled "Please! Make Me Over for My Class Reunion." In this article, women are chosen who plan to attend their tenth-, fifteenth-, twentieth-, and twenty-fifth-year reunions, and each is given concrete advice on make-up and hair so that they can be "Winners of our Reunion Makeover Contest." The most exhaustive advice was offered by free-lance writer Judy Markey in *Cosmopolitan* magazine. After discussing the negativism she felt about her own reunion, she outlined her "11-point program" for middle-aged women to make the most of a potentially traumatic reunion. Her advice, paraphrased below, reflects the kind of popular-cultural views on high school reunions that I have described:

"Cathy" © 1990, Cathy Guisewite, Universal Press Syndicate

1. When the invitation comes, and your trepidation threshold escalates, abandon all that knee-jerk negativism or should I / shouldn't I equivocation, and just GO.

2. Bring no spouse; bring no date.

3. Go with an old class friend.

4. Body preparation begins several months ahead.

5. Begin to prepare yourself mentally—on the informational and attitudinal levels. The latter includes avoiding the following poisonous mindsets: (a) *Gleeful curiosity about what the ravages of time have done to former prom queens and football captains*; (b) *The I'll-Show-Them-Syndrome*; (c) *The I Was Voted "Most Likely to Succeed" and Still Haven't Been on The Donahue Show Despair*; (d) *You were the class bitch, or bookworm, or black sheep, and they'll never let you forget it*; (e) *The unfinished business of unrequited sex.*

6. Be artful, and not too deceitful, with the information you submit to the Class Reunion Souvenir Book.

7. The Outfit—Something sartorially definitive of the woman you've become.

8. Take heart; also take your family photos and your business cards.

9. Conversation dos and don'ts: (a) *Don't obsessively announce how you've changed and/or were misunderstood*; (b) *Don't try to*

overimpress; it backfires; (c) *Don't make the direct inquiry "Are you married?"*; (d) *Don't get bogged down with the class schizoid*; (e) *Don't overextend yourself alcoholically or ingest undue amounts of illegal substances*; (f) *Do be lavish with deceitful exclamations like "You haven't changed at all!"*; (g) *Do seek out people peripheral to your high school experience, but pivotal to the preceding years*; (h) *Do demystify old demons.*

10. [Be careful with] nostalgic sex.

11. Find a group of people to leave with.[23]

Whenever I am home in Japan, I am always on the lookout for popular culture references to high school or high school reunions, but there does not seem to be a consistent cultural point of view of the kind we find in American popular culture. The class reunion (or encounters with ex–high school classmates) rarely appears as subject matter in Japanese popular culture, and when it does it is simply as a plot device with little significance in and of itself. For example, in a mystery novel by the popular author Seiichi Morimura, a professional thief attends his class reunion and obtains a list of potential victims—a booklet issued by the reunion committee containing former classmates' addresses. He then becomes involved in a series of homicides. I sought a cultural parallel, but the high school reunion was used by the author simply as one of many possible social settings in which the thief could obtain a list of addresses. His elaborate criminal scheme is independent of his experience in high school. Contrast this novel with an American mystery drama: An ex-football player (played by Rock Hudson) commits a series of murders in his search for a classmate who had written a prophecy just before their graduation that included predictions of what the graduates would become in the next twenty years. The motive for murder is to bury the record of the unfulfilled prophecy of the football player's life.[24]

There are more such examples in American popular culture than I could possibly mention, and their quantity and consistency attest to the power of high school symbolism and its associated cultural scenarios as a frame of reference for making sense of the life experiences of American adults. High school symbols are not neutral and abstract sources of meaning; they are concrete and provoke feelings. Each high school symbol embodies dramas that people experienced in their own high school days—dramas of success or failure in interpersonal relationships and the struggle for identity—involving joy, excitement, resentment, embarrassment, shame, and bitterness that shape, to a large extent, aspirations for adulthood. High school types portrayed in popular discourse could be one's high school friends, foes, heroes, heartthrobs—or even oneself. Stories of identity transformations, of late bloomers or fallen idols, besides satisfying adult curiosity about, say, "rejected cheerleaders" or "big, dumb jocks," impart a sense of delayed justice, assuring American adults that there is indeed life after high school, and providing cultural scenarios that form general expectations for post–high school life.

Thus, cultural discourse on high school provides a provocative "language school" for the ethnographer who does not intimately share the experiential and affective field of high school symbols and discourse. In this "school," one learns not only the grammar and cognitive association of words and references in high school language, but also, and more importantly, the "native's point of view"—not only coherence or intelligibility, but also what is worth laughing about, and what is worth being moved by. We will see how this point of view produces dramatic climaxes to the actual performances of class reunions, and how it takes diverse forms and colors in individual stories of high school and reunion experiences.

Methodological Perspective

AN ETHNOGRAPHY OF DISCOURSE

In the chapters that follow, I try to portray the drama of reunion events in a novelistic way, and present personal experiences as personal narratives. I attempt to capture in their immediacy the ways in which experience and sentiments take expression through such sense-making activities as ritual performances and story-tellings. Just as the participant-observer attempts to discover the ways people inhabit their cultural universe, the ethnographer of narrative tries also to "inhabit a discourse," to paraphrase Samuel Johnson. My goal is to reach out and feel, and to convey that feeling to the reader, to portray the "living universe" that is experienced through the sense-making activities of the people who inhabit it.[25]

The documentation of personal narratives has played a prominent role in the movement to construct new forms of ethnography.[26] Narratives—whether expressed in stories, life stories, anecdotes, commentary, or gossip—within and outside the reunion context are interpretive expressions of "life as experienced" (Bruner 1986). The inclusion of personal narratives in ethnographic accounts is considered by many to add new "life" to the presentation of ethnographic data and to give the routinized, rule-governed ethnographic present vitality and vibrancy. We have to move beyond the rules of the game, Renato Rosaldo (1986: 103) argues, to explore stories that other people tell themselves about themselves:

> In telling about a game do we want to know the rules or how it was played? Obviously both matter. And it makes no sense to throw out the baby with the bath water. But suppose for a moment that we try to learn only the rules of the game. Imagine, for example, the ethnographer returning from the last game of the World Series and reporting these remarkable discoveries: three strikes make an out, three outs retire the side, and so on. Eager to learn about every move in the game's key plays, the avid fan could only (correctly) say that the ethnographer was a fool who said nothing untrue but managed to miss the whole point of the game.

In my own ethnography, I try to go beyond the structure and functioning of reunions and the cognitive organization of reunion stories. Accordingly, I eschew an approach to interpretation that reduces the anthropological Other to alien "texts" to be intellectually "read," and try instead to grasp how sentiments are played and displayed in the dramatic form of reunion events and in personal narratives, and possibly even to reveal more about what makes life worth living than how it is lived.[27]

My ethnography of the high school reunion is based primarily on data pertaining to two types of sense-making activities: the collective and the individual. The first is derived from the documentation of the event as a whole, including: (1) the kinds of symbols selected to make a reunion frame; (2) the kinds of ceremonial events enacted; and (3) instances of situated storytelling and interactions between participants. In short, I study the ritual as a field of discourse—symbols and people in action in a social context.

My concept of discourse is derived mainly from Paul Ricoeur, who distinguished discourse from language as follows: (1) Discourse is always realized temporally and in the present, whereas a language system is virtual and outside of time; (2) language lacks a subject, whereas discourse is always self-referential; (3) discourse is always about something; (4) language is only the condition of communication, but it is in discourse that all messages are exchanged.

In reunion discourse, semantically rich, and often emotionally charged, messages are communicated in a manner that looks to an outsider like a "telegraphic shorthand" (R. Rosaldo 1986: 108). Symbols used in the discourse are rooted in past experience. References to particular high school events or episodes remind participants of a dramatic sequence in which they participated, or of the name of a former classmate that embodies an image of his adolescent self and his life story as created in part by his classmates. Furthermore, high school symbols may mean different things to different participants—e.g., "cheerleader tryout" means different things to a cheerleader selected than to a cheerleader rejected. The meaning of such symbols depends largely upon the subjective stance individuals take toward their high school experiences at the time of the reunion. Symbols are affective, for people not only attribute meanings to symbols but also experience them as a driving force (Turner) or as motive (Burke) and use them in figurative ways to obtain certain results in situated contexts. Special attention is given to the layering of experience, symbols for experience, and attribution of multiple meanings to symbols (Turner).

The second sort of data I have drawn on—the sense-making activities of the individual—concerns the meaning of a particular reunion in the unfolding biography of a specific individual—i.e., how the event is received by the consciousness and how the interpretation of the experience is incorporated into the ongoing process of making sense. The stories presented do not cover the "whole" life story of particular people,[28] but are thematic in character; they contain substories that focus on the place of high school and class reunions in the interviewee's life.

Life-story narratives have been considered effective in that: (1) they can throw light on the subjective side of a culture, enhancing a more generalized ethnography; (2) they can elucidate the inner processes of an individual; (3) they can focus on the way an individual interacts with society; and (4) they can incorporate time depth, which is usually unattainable in a short period of fieldwork. The prominent shortcomings of earlier approaches to life history, however, were the naive assumptions that life history data *directly* represent an individual life, and that one carries one's life history in one's head, ready to be *discovered* when an ethnographer approaches it with the proper techniques. However, this putative self-evident nature of life histories has come under critical scrutiny. The context of the interview and the relationship between informant and ethnographer are now held to constitute an important aspect of the ethnographic data material.[29]

The life stories in my ethnography are significantly different from the narratives I collected at reunions, in that the narrative frames of the former were established by the ethnographer, not the informants themselves. Life-story narratives were collected in guided interviews in which the narratives were constructed with the ethnographer through the interactive process of questions and answers. The interviews were arranged to be as close as possible to ordinary conversation: I neither took notes nor used a structured questionnaire, but instead used a tape recorder and mental notes. Conversation was allowed and encouraged to flow freely in accordance with what the interviewees wanted to discuss. Both the ethnographer's and interviewee's points of view were operating as stories were elicited. The stories, therefore, should be viewed as what Gelya Frank (1979) calls a "double biography" in the sense that they are the outcome of an interplay between interviewer and interviewee. The ethnographer guides the way interviewees reflect upon their life experiences. Storytelling takes into account the audience's (in this case, the ethnographer's) reactions, which are influenced by the ethnographer's own life experiences and cultural knowledge (e.g., "You are still young so you haven't experienced it, but . . ." or "You are Japanese so you don't know what Sadie Hawkins is, do you?"). In the process of interacting with the Japanese interviewer, the interviewees developed a good sense of what she did and did not know, and used that emergent intuition in deciding whether to supply more cultural and group-specific information.

One of my key aims in employing an ethnography of discourse is representing the diversity within a culture and foregrounding individual action and experience. High school reunions, to borrow Clifford's phrase, are a "carnivalesque area of diversity" (1988: 46), where the different life experiences of former classmates intersect. People act and react to the ritual event, and incorporate their experiences into their consciousness differently. A ritual event may mean different things to different people, and naturally their interpretations differ. And sometimes they confront each other.

The notion of diversity, in the sense intended here, is derived from the phenomenologists' concept of the relativity of subjective experience and the individual's point of view (James), the special kind of connection between expression and experience (Dilthey), the process in which subjective realities, or private interpretation, become an "objective" reality (Berger and Luckman), or collective interpretation, and vice versa. This view posits that a culture is multifaceted, multilayered, and open-ended. Just as studying cultural realities is like looking through a kaleidoscope, with each turn bringing out a new configuration and reality, the kind of ethnography employed here allows different readings. Thus, in contrast to a kind of ethnography in which the anthropologist summarizes, generalizes, and paraphrases the bulk of her interview data, the stories here, while selected and edited by me, are told by multiple voices, including my own. In presenting "speaking subjects in a field of multiple discourses" (Clifford 1988: 46), I hope this ethnography will allow the American reader to examine and evaluate one Japanese interpretation of certain American events and experiences.

FIELDWORK

The major part of my fieldwork was carried out between 1982 and 1984, while I was a graduate student at the University of Illinois. Because of the nature of the topic, nearly every American I interacted with was a potential informant. Some valuable information was collected from everyday conversations, gossip, popular magazines, television programs, and newspapers. Some of my professors, colleagues, and friends volunteered to be interviewed about their previous reunion experiences, and some others invited me to reunions they were attending. Through personal contacts, I attended reunions in a small, rural community in Minnesota, in a New York suburb, in Chicago, and in a satellite town of Champaign-Urbana. These provided a good comparative perspective on the reunions of Elm High School in Champaign-Urbana, which were the main focus of my research.

I attended eight reunions in the Champaign-Urbana area. Two of these (a fifth- and a fiftieth-year reunion) were the reunions of classes from Oak High School, and the rest (tenth, fifteenth, twentieth, thirtieth, fortieth, and fiftieth years) were of Elm High School graduates. In three of the Champaign-Urbana reunions (in the tenth-, twentieth- and fortieth-year reunions of Elm High School), I observed the committee meetings held before and after the reunions.

First contacts with reunion organizers were made by responding to reunion announcements in the local newspaper. I sent a letter introducing myself and my project to the person listed in the advertisement for former classmates to contact. A couple of days after the estimated delivery date of my letter, I contacted the person again by phone. Usually I was asked to wait for another week or two until there had been another committee meeting, at which the possibility of my attendance could be discussed. Generally speaking, younger classes had a more casual attitude toward this intruder, but as the age of the alumni increased, the decision on whether to allow an outsider, though eventually positive, was handled more cautiously. Here is a typical reaction I received from an older reunion organizer: "Personally, I don't see any reason why not. But this is a *very* private gathering. Just old people, just our classmates and their spouses. I'm afraid they may feel awkward to have anybody else. I'll address this in the next committee meeting and let you know."

The reunion is typically a closed gathering at which attendance is limited to former classmates, their spouses, and invited guests, such as former teachers. Although I tried to keep a low profile at reunions to minimize any effect on the natural unfolding of the event, keeping my anonymity was difficult. In reunions beyond the thirtieth year, I was introduced formally as a guest, with the Master of Ceremonies describing the purpose of my presence (see Chapter 5). In the reunions of younger people, on the other hand, I was not introduced formally, and a lot of people were puzzled by my presence and wondered whether there had been a Japanese American in their class whom they could not recognize. Some people asked straightforwardly whose wife I was. But as the evening progressed, word of mouth spread rapidly and most of the reuniters knew the purpose of my presence. I did talk with people at the reunion, but I concentrated more on observation and recording, and making contacts with people, rather than launching into extensive interviews on the spot, so that people's experience would be minimally affected by my intrusion.

Equipped with a camera, tape recorder, and notebook, I was often taken by reunion attendees to be a reporter from a local newspaper (see Chapter 5). Upon learning that I was not a reporter, who might bring instant attention to the class and its reunion, some participants seemed relieved and others disappointed. Then sometimes they assigned me, informally through casual conversation, the role of "recorder" of their reunions. I gladly took on this assignment, and offered copies of my tapes and pictures to the people who wanted them. The slides I took at reunions, in particular, created opportunities for more interviews and observation. After the reunions, I conducted interviews with informants individually while looking over the slides with them. I was also invited to the postreunion meetings of organizers to show my slides. These occasions not only provided me with more detailed information about what was going on at the reunion as seen by the participants, but also helped me to grasp which aspects of the reunion most appealed to participants, cognitively and emotionally. The "native's point of view" that I gained in this manner helped shape the final ethnography. Interestingly, in most cases the organizers asked to have copies of my slides to show at the next reunion. The ethnographer's "data" became part of the "official" class history.

Initially, I planned to obtain a well-balanced sample of the people from each high school class for my life-history interviews. One of the questions I was interested in was whether reunions have different meanings to people with different biographical experiences after graduation, and what variables would account for that difference. For example, is there any significant difference between the people who come from afar to attend the reunions and those who did not move away from the town where they grew up? The most frustrating aspect of my research was inherent in the phenomenon I studied. The reunion class, as I mentioned earlier, does not exist as a concrete group in a specific locality. It is a group of people who gather only in the context of reunions, and, as I will discuss later, they do not usually interact with one another in their everyday life, as they used to in high school, even if they live in the same town.

I could obtain more in-depth interviews with people who were current residents of Champaign-Urbana because, without exception, people who came from out of town went home almost immediately after the event, and some potentially fascinating informants—such as the women introduced in the Preface—returned to places I could not afford to visit: San Francisco, Florida, even Thailand.

When I traveled to other cities with my Champaign-Urbana informants to attend their reunions, I was faced with a different kind of frustration. Because of limitations on the time I could take off from school, I could interview only a limited number of people while I was there; only one informant came home with me to Champaign-Urbana for a more intensive life-story interview.

In the end, I interviewed more than sixty people, twenty of whom agreed to grant in-depth, life-story interviews. For the logistical reasons noted above, most of the life-story interviews were done with residents of Champaign-Urbana. Although I could not compare home-comers with home-stayers in a controlled manner, I obtained a comparative sample through Champaign-Urbana residents who attended out-of-town reunions, with or without my company.

Another kind of bias in my sample of informants stems from variation in the willingness and accessibility of informants. Sometimes they were influenced by my association with particular classmates. Since I usually made my first contacts with the high school class through the reunion organizers, I found it difficult to cross the boundaries of their social relationships with former classmates. The topic of high school, and especially that of high school classmates and what had become of them after school, was a sensitive subject. Sometimes valuable information was picked up from gossip and bad-mouthing. But once people agreed to be interviewed, I found my position as an outsider rather advantageous. The interviewees felt relatively free to express negative sentiments about others that were usually suppressed for reasons of interpersonal etiquette. In this sense, the relationship with the outsider was one of intimacy, in which one could confide "true feelings" that were not normally revealed in other social contexts.[30]

Unknowingly, but perhaps inevitably, I sometimes intruded into the most private areas of people's lives. There were several instances in which I had to discontinue or redirect interviews. For example, when I asked in an interview with the chairman of the fiftieth-year reunion of Elm High School about the most memorable thing he recalled from his high school days, I was stunned to see tears start running down the face of this sixty-eight-year-old company president. Trying to compose himself, he told me that the most memorable thing was meeting his wife, and that he had just learned she was dying of cancer. "So this will be the last reunion for us." He had been Class President and she was Homecoming Queen, and together they had been organizing reunions every ten years since graduation. They would have been the "ideal" American couple to include in my ethnography. In such instances, though the ethnographer in me wanted to know more, simple decency dictated that I not unnecessarily disturb such critical moments in potential informants' lives.

The most difficult decision to make was choosing which reunion stories to retell in full in my ethnography. In order to maintain a sense of controlled comparison, my main focus is on the reunions and graduates of Elm High School in Champaign-Urbana. Full descriptions of the reunions of two graduating classes appear in Chapter 3 (the tenth-year reunion of the Class of '72) and Chapter 5 (the fortieth-year reunion of the Class of '42); the protagonists of the life stories presented in Chapter 4 are participants selected from the tenth-year reunion of the Elm High Class of '72. As the stories of events and lives unfold, the reader will gain a sense of the relationship between individual stories and class reunions, and a sense of time—both lifecourse and historical—operating in the organization of events and in the autobiographies of individuals who graduated from the same high school.

Since my goal as a Japanese ethnographer was to portray "ordinary American experience," the life stories presented are "ordinary" in the sense that I heard similar stories throughout the course of my research, and that the tellers were well-adjusted, "healthy" individuals who were not facing any unusual psychological problems at the time of the interview. However, the stories should not be regarded as "typical" or "representative." Any single life cannot represent others in the same high school class or age-cohort. Each story should be read in its own right. Each of us weaves meanings into and out of unique life experiences and relates them to specific social and historical currents. In each telling, we strive to achieve coherence in order to account for a unique self. Each reunion story is a personal account, but its construction is also a social action.[31]

Edward Sapir once wrote: "Under familiar circumstances and with familiar people, the locus of reference of our interest is likely to be to the individual. In unfamiliar types of behavior . . . the interest tends to discharge itself into formulations which are cultural rather than personal in character" (1956: 194). Given my peculiar point of view—that of a Japanese who had lived in Champaign-Urbana for an extended period of time—my ethnographic interest oscillated between the cultural patterning of a ritual event (high school reunions), the "personal" way an event materializes, and "individual" modes of interpretation.

The organization of this book reflects these mixed concerns. First, if you will allow the cinematic metaphor, I will present a wide-angle "establishing shot" of reunions in America, elucidating the characteristic features of this ritual and discussing the essential processes that generate reflexivity. Then I will zoom in, to examine the way in which meaning is collectively constructed in a specific reunion. Next, I present close-ups of two reunion participants and demonstrate how the reunion intersects with their individual biographies. Finally, I pull back again, discussing the time patterning of reunions throughout the life-course, and trying ultimately to identify the significance of high school reunions for American adulthood.

2 How Reunions Work

We must find our separate meaning
In the persuasion of our days
Until we meet in the meaning of the world.

—*Christopher Fry,* The Firstborn

The high school reunion is a secular ritual that provides a setting for collective reflexivity. It offers participants the opportunity to tell and reflect upon their lives, and in the process they may also construct new stories about their lives. Such stories may in turn serve as guiding metaphors for editing and re-editing the "biography of the self."

The biography of the self refers to the subjective aspect of the life-course that involves reflexive actions through which one comes to know oneself. One's lifecourse is an ongoing process of self-construction, in which one strives toward one's own integrity by organizing and re-organizing one's relations to others through the medium of symbolic actions. As a person composes a biography of the self, past experience does not exist as a fixed entity frozen in memory but is in flux, being continuously and figuratively transformed to reconstruct, or to recon-firm, a sense of self at the present point in time and to orient oneself to the future. Does the experience of attending a high school reunion affect these processes of constructing a biography of the self? The issue here is one of linkages between ritual events and the construction of the self.

High school reunions, like other rituals, are framed events. The reunion provides a frame for (1) collective discourse, a social occasion to tell and hear life stories, and (2) a collective journey to the past. A high school reunion creates, in the flow of everyday life, a symbolic environment in which two distinct experiential communities are brought into contact: (1) the community that was shared in high school days but no longer exists in the everyday present, and (2) the community that emerges in the reunion, consisting of people with a sense of a shared past but without a sense of a shared everyday present. I see this symbolic duality as the basic experiential structure that generates collective reflexivity. The overwhelming task of the reunion is not only to reflect and organize group consciousness, but more significantly to generate meanings and shape the direction of interpretive actions by which collective and individual biographies are constructed.

In this chapter, I will first discuss the theoretical background of biography of the self and reflexivity, present an overview of the common experiential structure of reunion as a ritual, and then explore the ways in which reunions foster reflexivity and create meaning.

Biography of the Self

I derived my notion of biography of the self and reflexivity primarily from George Herbert Mead and Wilhelm Dilthey. For Mead, the self is a social entity that emerges, forms, and re-forms in reflexive discourse. The self is an active agent endowed with the power of symbolic communication through which one can rhetorically transform the world in which one lives. The unique capacity of the self is its ability to differentiate and to enter into a discourse with "I"—spontaneous individuality not yet objectified in consciousness, and "Me"—objectified and internalized experiences and social expectations. The self is the reflective mind, for it takes the inner drives, motives, feelings, and perceived cultural and social realities—in short, the lived experience—as "objects," or signs for interpretation. In Mead's words, "the self can become an object to itself." It is through this reflexive discourse with ourselves and others that we gain "*le sens du 'moi'*" (Mauss 1938), and experience ourselves as a "unified being." Reflexivity, in Mead's view, "is the essential condition within the social process for the development of mind" (1962: 134).

Mead saw the social action or the experience of the self as being in a continuous temporal flow of "before" and "after"—the present is continuously sinking into the past while the previously uncertain future is turning into another concrete present. And a past takes on significance only in the context of the present. The past must be found in the present world only in its representation in memory (1962: 116, 351). And our memories are organized "upon the string of our self" (1962: 135). In Mead's view, experience comes to have meaning only when it is identified with significant symbols. It is through objectification that meaning develops into its highest and most complex form and becomes part of human consciousness. Mead, however, left us with a question: How does meaning become organized in a way that produces a sense of integrity?

Like Dilthey, I maintain that a person's lifecourse is a continuous process of constructing meaning that can connect the past to the present, and the present to the anticipated future. For Dilthey, meaning is the most comprehensive category "through which life becomes comprehensible" (1961: 105). He distinguished "meaning" from "value," and described life as "an infinite multiplicity of positive and negative existential values," which have no fixed relationships to one another. "It is like a chaos of chords and discords. Each is a structure of notes which fills a present but has no musical relation to the others" (p. 104). Meaning is achieved when a connection is discovered between past and present experience and a "musical relationship" is established by the conscious mind. Further, the "meaning" so established is never fixed, because "living through an experience calls for ever new links" (p. 102), and this often entails a new interpretation of the past. Or sometimes a past experience that has been subsumed or "forgotten" is revived and prompts us to reorganize and to create a new musical relationship. Like Mead, Dilthey saw that the past is never fixed, and that it is "my perception of life in the present" that creates meaning for one's life.

The philosophical views of Dilthey and Mead are supported by scholars who study human development and psychology. Bernice Neugarten, who studies human development over the lifecourse, finds that one unique feature of an adult is that he or she is a "self-propelling individual," characterized by a "highly refined power of introspection and reflection," and "continually busying himself in making a coherent story out of his life history" (1969: 23). Experimental psychologists suggest that throughout adulthood, earlier memories are continually revised as a function of subsequent experience.[1] Theories of memory also suggest the view that new information leads to transformation of the previous pattern of memories.[2]

A person's lifecourse and its integration cannot be seen only as successive reintegrations of new experiences and change. The biography of the self is transformative as well as integrative. We select from past experiences or past images of the self represented in memory, and continuously reinterpret them and reassess their significance in order to create a "new edition" of our life. In short, the construction of a biography of the self is a lifelong process of organization and reorganization of meaning achieved by reflexive evaluations of experience through which we gain an integral self and an orientation toward the future.

"Biography of the self" may be conceived in more commonly used terms, such as self-awareness or self-image. I use "biography of the self" to refer to the unique centrality of a person, in an effort to overcome the shortcomings of these more familiar concepts. First, the phrase corrects the passive nature of such concepts by establishing that *le sens du moi* is simultaneously both creative agent and the product of a reflexive discourse. And second, the phrase revises the static and timeless notions of self-concept by focusing on the process of construction, which inevitably involves a dialectical interplay of past, present, and future.

In everyday life, however, the construction of the biography of the self is more or less routinized and unmarked in interactions with taken-for-granted others in familiar settings. We tend to repeat a standard version of self, so to speak, to people with whom we interact on an everyday basis. As Bertram Cohler points out (1982), through continuing reconstructive activities leading to the maintenance of a particular personal narrative of our lives, a sense of stability and consistency is experienced in everyday life. Thus, once a standard version of the self is formed and is validated and objectified in social interactions, the story becomes a reality for oneself and others. As we act out the standard biography of the self, our self-image tends to be reaffirmed and maintained.

The high school reunion interrupts this ongoing flow of everyday routine, and calls attention to the habitual acts of creating the biography of the self by bringing a particular past (i.e., high school days) back into focus in our present lives. In storytelling, enactment, and performance, this secular ritual creates a powerful experiential environment that promotes reflexive impulses. In the next section, I show how a symbolic duality of past and present materializes in the reunion and works to become a catalyst for reflexivity.

The Event

The reunion experience, or meeting one's past, does not begin and end with the event. For program organizers, it begins about a year before, when they start the preparations, and for others it begins when they receive the reunion announcement. People often express complex feelings, for the announcement not only brings back high school memories that have been relegated to peripheral consciousness, but reminds them of the passage of time, drawing attention to now and then, and to what has happened in between.

Silvia Klapes, a housewife who was contemplating her twentieth-year reunion, expressed her apprehension before the event:

> It was really a weird feeling. When I found that little letter in the mailbox, I said to myself, "I can't believe it's been twenty years!" It brought back all those memories from school, all those familiar faces I now only see in my yearbook. My immediate reaction was very positive. I was very interested, I thought, in going to see how all the others are doing now. But later I felt reluctant. As the reunion date approached, I was sort of depressed. I wondered how they'd react to me. I started to think about what I've been doing for the last twenty years.

Margie Steward recalled receiving an invitation to a reunion of her high school class of '67:

> I had seldom thought about high school and about those people from school until I received that invitation. I live away from home now and do not keep in touch with high school friends. I didn't care much about those people in school. So part of me wanted to go and say: "Hey, I've made it!" because I know that they didn't ex-

pect a career woman from a shy high school girl. But part of me said, "What if they don't remember me? Why should I bother to see them and prove myself to people who couldn't care less?" I agonized for about a month before I finally decided, "What the heck."

A reunion is, by its nature, a voluntary meeting; no one has to attend. Yet it is common to observe reluctance even among those who decide to go. The source of reluctance is mainly "unpredictability." As Jim Crouse, an active member of the reunion committee of the Elm High Class of '42, put it, "You don't know who is coming, you don't know how much they have changed, you don't know how they will treat you now. You just don't know what you can expect! I wondered if the stuck-up ones would still be stuck-up."

There are two key reasons people give for attending their reunions: One is curiosity about what has happened to their old classmates, and about how they rank among their classmates. Another is to show off the adult selves they have achieved. Often these two motivations are closely related, as we can see in the following explanation Mrs. Brown gave for her husband's attending his twentieth-year reunion. "The only reason my husband went back to his class reunion was to show off that he made it when some of the others thought that they were a lot better. His folks didn't have anything, his mother was married two or three times. He didn't want to be remembered as he was then. It was his ego trip, too—he wanted to find out how he compares now."

High school reunions are attended by willing participants. Some participants prepare themselves for the reunion by studying their high school yearbook to polish up their memory of their high school days and friends. Others deliberately make an effort to improve or manipulate their appearance or their image, knowing that life stories are told not only through the verbal medium but also the visual. Many people go on a diet, or buy new outfits for this special occasion, and several informants spoke of acquaintances who had actually had a face-lift for a reunion.

One graduate student went back to her tenth-year reunion in a short black skirt and new haircut expressly to make the statement that she was not married, was pursuing an academic career, and had not "sold out like the other cheerleaders," whom she had expected to have become wives and mothers. "For the reunion, I dressed with a great deal of care but also for the purpose of making my very own statement. I thought it's also significant that I was sending messages to myself at the same time," said one forty-seven-year-old woman. For her the task of presentation of self was complicated because the way she dressed simultaneously affected herself and her husband, who had graduated with the same high school class. "I enjoy doing needlework and am very much interested in folk art, so I wore a patchwork dress with an orange bodice that I had made. And what else can you wear with patchwork? I wore a mink stole, my diamond earrings, and my diamond ring!" She improvised this unique combination in order to accommodate the impression her husband wanted to convey about himself. "My husband was very distraught because he thought my patches reflected poorly on him. In order to salvage his ego, I said, 'All right, I am going to wear my patchwork dress no matter what, but I'll also wear the mink stole and the diamonds so that people will see I have them, if that will make you feel better.' So I did and it was fun. I think it might have been one of the first times I realized how much I enjoy dressing up to create a particular effect."

High school reunions are held only upon the initiative of individual men and women who venture to be program organizers. Arrangements for the meeting are totally up to the organizers. But the following are the dominant events that characterize the gathering as an experience of being united.

"One of the most salient characteristics of ritual," Barbara Myerhoff and Sally Moore (1977) have noted, "is its function as a frame."[3] The symbols are the creative agent of the framing; they transform a sector of spatial and temporal reality into "something different" from everyday routine. In reunions the symbols that constitute the frame are taken from high school days. The school banner is almost always present. Colors used to decorate the meeting place are the high school's colors. Sometimes the total arrangement of the setting generates an atmosphere that resembles popular events in high school—such as proms or school-auditorium dances. Old songs, such as fight songs or cheer songs, are played; old newspaper clips, cheerleaders' costumes, and old pictures are displayed. These symbols, when selected and combined together, create a context in which time is bridged—from the present to the past and back again.

What belongs to the past, however, can never be reinstated exactly as it was (Schutz 1945). The past generated in this ritual frame is, in fact, a "fiction." Familiar faces last seen as teenagers now appear as adult strangers. So during the cocktail hour, which the organizers call an "ice-breaker," feelings of do-they-remember-me or do-I-recognize-them are prevalent, and it is not rare to observe reunion participants spending a lot of time squinting at one another's chests to read name tags, or playing identity guessing games. In some reunions, the "ice-breaker" is carefully arranged to occur the night before the event in order to facilitate the transition to "yesteryear."

After the "ice-breaker" there is a dinner, followed by a formal program, which consists of speeches, award-giving, honoring of the dead, and introducing those who have served on the reunion committee.

Award-giving is a ceremonial event that is widely practiced and is often the most remembered event of a reunion. Awards are based on data gathered by the organizers through questionnaires they send out with the reunion announcements. Questionnaires cover major accomplishments in life, such as education, career, marriage, children, where you live, and how far you have traveled. Sometimes the data collected are distributed to the participants in the form of statistics; in one reunion the organizers published a booklet in which they laid out the original senior class pictures with short statements below them reporting later achievements. Reunion awards are given for activities and markers related to transitions in the life cycle, for example, Longest Married, Most Recently Married, Most Times Married, Most Children, and Most Grandchildren. Biological changes, too, are recognized, such as Most Gray Hair, Baldest, Most Well-Kept Figure, Most Changed, and Least Changed.

This ritual—award-giving—is a re-creation of a common high school practice, but the content reflects and epitomizes the present condition of participants. Naturally, the kinds of award given vary with the year of the reunion. For example, awards such as the Most Eligible Man or Woman appear in the tenth year, and the Most Well-Kept Figure or Baldest appear after the twentieth year.

A popular award that does not fall into either of the previous categories is the Farthest Traveled. This award recognizes the spatial mobility of people who started out from the same place at the same time. Simultaneously, it celebrates the importance of making an effort to be united again.

The chief entertainment of any reunion, however, is talking and gossiping. The reunion participants mingle, reminiscing and exchanging postgraduation biographies. Usually a band or some form of music is provided so that people can dance, but dancing seems to be the least popular reunion activity.

Although reminiscing is a crucial element of reunions—particularly, as we shall see in Chapter 5, those of older generations—most attendees prefer talking about the present to reminiscing about the past. They talk about what they do and why, and what has happened to them since graduation, their marriages, children, work, and deaths in the family. They comment to one another on whether or not they have changed. And just as the kinds of awards given change with the number of years that have elapsed since graduation, so do the main topics of conversation. Thus, marriage and jobs are the central topics on the tenth anniversary, whereas retirement and taking care of one's parents, as well as the marriages of one's children and grandchildren, are the most frequently discussed topics at the thirtieth-year and later reunions. Furthermore, the discourse in this ritual frame is not free from the wider sociohistorical context in which it occurs.

The effect of reunion extends beyond the ritual frame. Elaine, who attended a "war-years" reunion (the war in question being World War II) wearing a cheerleader's uniform—even though, or perhaps because, she had never been a cheerleader—had this to say after the event: "I couldn't get to sleep last night. I couldn't fall asleep because the faces, like a moving picture camera, kept going past my eyes. I kept thinking to myself, 'Oh my god, I can't believe I saw this one and that one . . .' You know? I was restless thinking about that." A college professor who went back to his thirty-fifth reunion commented: "The reunion took a certain amount out of me emotionally. At the end of the day I was incredibly exhausted. And when I came back, it took me a couple of days before I could sort of free my mind of these things and go back to ordinary concerns back home. It really was a sort of emotionally taxing experience."

Introspection and reflection on one's life seem to continue after the reunion is over. "Since the reunion, I came to spend more time thinking about my life, because, you know, it made me feel middle-aged for the first time," recalled one high school teacher. "I'm in an occupation where I see mostly younger people. Of course I see people as old as I am at work and also I have friends of my own age, but I've known them [people at her reunion] for twenty to twenty-five years. So seeing them getting older was somehow a depressing experience. I thought that I had done relatively well, but, you know, if they look old to me, I must look old to them." "The reunion was pivotal," another woman recalled of her twentieth-year reunion held seven years earlier. "In a sense, it forced me to reassess my life." Soon after the reunion she was divorced, went back to school, and developed a new career as an interior designer. Although the instances in which the reunion acts as the catalyst for major life changes are rare, many people report experiencing a reflexive impulse after the reunion. What generates such emotional currents and sparks?

Reflexivity

One of the paramount roles of high school reunions is to establish a cultural frame for telling life stories. The telling (or writing) of one's life evokes far more powerful reflexive activity than that which goes on in everyday life, and is, as Dilthey points out, "the highest and most instructive form in which the understanding of life confronts us" (1961: 85–87). The telling of a life story is not merely a report; a story can never be a complete duplication of actual events. Telling is a conscious process of giving meaning to, or of reorganizing, personal events in a way that transmutes them into experience and allocates them to a definite place in consciousness. Linguistic activity as such is a reflexive action. First, telling involves a shuttle movement between our recollection of what has happened and the existing symbol system; we must look back and search for a meaning from the system that fits our story and our purpose in telling it. Telling is not simply the automatic application of meanings from the conventional symbol system; in order to make our story plausible the meanings have to be rooted in shared symbols and must follow the cultural convention of "intelligibility"

(Ricoeur 1977). Second, telling is not unidirectional communication; we need audiences, both inner (self) and outer (others). Our telling has to take into account the reactions of these two audiences. During this process, actions are often transformed so as to construct a story that integrates them into our self-conception.

A high school reunion provides a unique audience: high school classmates. They were once powerful forces in shaping our self-image, but now they only remember us as we were. In terms of our current biography of the self, they may be less important than present significant others and may function only as "a sort of chorus" (Berger and Luckman 1967). But in the reunion this precedence is reversed. In each meeting with former classmates, we are forced, in the privacy of our minds or in conversation, to face our high school self as it is remembered by classmates.

A graduate student related a painful experience her high school friend Jim had at their tenth-year reunion:

> I went home early because Jim dragged me out of there. He just felt completely uncomfortable. He really felt like old wounds were being dredged up because people had a real stereotyped idea of him. People remember him as being this complete hippie, drug-scene type, and he wasn't at all—it was just because it was kind of a conservative school, and he always felt that he'd been misunderstood and maligned by people. So in the beginning, when we first went in, he changed the name [on his tag] and right away he set that whole feeling up and he just confirmed it and then they confirmed it right back, so he just felt like, "Wow."

A business student experienced a similar frustration at her fifteenth-year reunion. "At the time of my fifteenth-year reunion, I was just graduating from business school and I was very excited about it. So I was telling this classmate of mine what I have been doing, about friends at school, and all that. Then, she asked me, 'Do you tell your friends there that you were a cheerleader?' I thought 'Give me a break!' I thought I had buried that image a long time ago. So I had to tell her all the things that had happened to me after school."

At the reunion our stories have to deal simultaneously with the present self and the remembered self in a way that confirms the changes and continuities in our current self-identification. We have to work out discrepancies between the remembered self reflected in others' minds and the present self in our own mind. This "double encounter with past and present identity" (Plath 1980: 226) enhances the sense of reflexivity, possibly up to the point of creating a new story, certainly to the point of amending our self-image. It may be possible to obtain this experiential duality in other settings than reunions, but sporadic encounters with long-time friends may not be intense enough to condense the reflexive impulse into a powerful motive for confirming or revising the current biography of the self.

Marjorie Grady, a forty-seven-year-old housewife who runs a day-care center in her house, is one of the people who admit that her self-image changed after the reunion.

> I don't know if the reunion affected me so much, but I do know that my self-image changed after that. I had this feeling all along that high school had been a nightmare. I was marginal in all respects. I was very insecure. But at the reunion, everybody remembered me. Some people even talked to me about the one and only time I had made the honor roll, and the article I had written for the school paper. Some men even joked that they had wanted to ask me to marry them. People were coming over to me and saying, "Come on over to my table." I felt good about myself.

At a reunion, the participant's image of herself is suspended and bracketed in encountering the people whose memories of her high-school self may be different from her own. The new self-awareness gained through such a reflexive discourse becomes a reality that is incorporated into her self-concept.

Thus far I have considered reflexivity from the storyteller's perspective. There is another aspect of the collective discourse of the reunion that is equally important. That is, the tellers are listeners at the same time. The high school reunion constitutes one of those very rare and intense occasions on which we encounter numerous stories of others' lives. If, to use James Olney's terminology, tellers are "autobiographers" who are busily working "teleologically" to come to terms with past and present selves from their present (i.e., adult) perspective, listeners, on the other hand, are "biographers," "ontogenetically" seeking patterns in the life trajectories of others based on the remembered past (Olney 1980). That is, the listener's point of view is set to see what type of "kids" turned out to be what kind of adults and to look for causal links between the past and the present. One good example is a comment made by Joan Miller, a career woman, about her fifteenth-year reunion in California:

> The people who were very outgoing and the cheerleader types were still doing the cheerleading kinds of things. One of them had opened a diet and health center and now is cheering people on to lose weight and trim their bodies.
>
> The people who I found dull and boring were still dull and boring, with only one or two exceptions. There was one man in our class who talked ad infinitum, and I was very pleased to learn that he had become an attorney. I thought that was exactly what he needed to do. He would argue about anything, for any reason, without knowing anything at all about it! And he hadn't changed at all.
>
> There were a few surprises—people who had been very quiet, and not at all outgoing, had become very active. One of them just barely squeaked through high school. He was always drawing and had a very funny, devastating wit. He is now a cartoonist for Disney and had worked previously for Hanna-Barbera [another animation studio]. He was much more outspoken than he had ever been. I think he'd developed a sense of self-confidence. He was as witty verbally as he had always been in his cartoons.
>
> The jocks seemed to have the most trouble. A lot of them had been married and divorced, some several times. It seemed that those people who were used to having a lot of attention in high school tended to go into sales-type jobs. During the sixties, this country was up and down as far as the economy was concerned, and I think that must have been very difficult for them.
>
> The people who had been particularly brainy seemed to continue to be brainy. There were two medical doctors, several lawyers, and several Ph.D.'s. It was really a surprise to me because they were such a cross-section of the general American population. There were some kids who came from farms, some kids whose parents were managers, some were professional, lots of blue collar workers.

Surely, the ex-classmates discussed in the above narrative may perceive their life trajectories quite differently than this "biographer" does. For example, the woman who runs the health center may not see her occupation as a continuation of cheerleading, and the cartoonist may see his present success as a natural outgrowth of his high school role as a local wit.

However, the biographer elucidates a story line that brings into relief the high school image of the classmates, and by contrasting what she remembers about the classmates with what she perceives the classmates to be now, she discerns changes and continuities in their life trajectories. What is unique about the point of view of the biographer is that it not only compares and contrasts, but also tends to seek an "understanding" of others' lives by trying to discover causal links. For example, "those who are used to having a lot of attention in high school ended up becoming local salesmen," but "it could have been the way the economy was back then."

By listening to stories of others' lives that have "a shared beginning" (i.e., high school) but unfold differently, the participants may identify a historical or social force that they themselves may or may not have experienced equally. One of my informants, Sharon, said: "In the reunion, I found that three of our classmates were killed in the Vietnam War, one of whom, as a matter of fact, was my high school sweetheart, whom I almost married. My life would have been so much different if I had married him." John, who went to his tenth-year reunion (see Chapters 3 and 4), said: "Talking to other people at the reunion, you find that the economy looks pretty bad everywhere. A lot of people, even those who were considered to be most successful, are not real satisfied, so in a way I was a little more satisfied with the fact, knowing that other people are in the same boat."

They may also ascertain that other classmates are in the same life stage they are. After his thirtieth-year reunion, one businessman commented:

> One of the things that struck me in particular at the reunion was how old everybody was. I've been told by some people that when they go to a reunion, it's so depressing. I didn't find it that way at all. But I was impressed by the fact that they looked very much like

middle-aged people. Older people. Of course, as I remembered them, they were children in high school. And of course intellectually I knew that they would grow old, but somehow I couldn't imagine how they would look. Seeing them get old made me feel middle-aged for the first time.

The reunion participants, while reading out others' unfolding biographies, derive meanings from them and elaborate and enrich their own biographies with a sense of history, a sense of mortality, and an articulation of where they are in their lifecourse relative to those of others. The reunion links individual biography with cohort story and with larger social-historical currents.

This process is highlighted in ceremonial events, such as award-giving or honoring the dead. These events call people's attention to a standard or "official" version of the story of "our class"—where they started, where they are, and what they do, as well as where they are going. Through these processes of storytelling and ritual enactments, participants come to abstract "A Story of Our Class," which epitomizes the present span of participants' lives. This in turn constitutes a "narrative scale" by which participants measure their present selves and evaluate whether they are ahead or behind, and from which they gain a sense of affirmation about where and what they are now, and legitimizes what they are going to do. Susan, who attended her fifteenth-year reunion, said: "In the reunion, I was very impressed by the number of women who had recently returned to school. Because at that time I was studying by myself to go to college in the fall. In my small rural neighborhood, women of my age, most of them were housewives. I had been feeling that I might be a little strange, or too 'liberated' or, as we used to say in school, 'queer.'" Another woman, Mrs. Thompson, found in her fiftieth-year reunion that she was not the only one who had to take care of very aged parents. "When Harold [the Master of Ceremonies] asked people to raise their hands if they were taking care of their parents, I thought I would be one of a few. I was very surprised that there were so many people like me. I always felt that I was becoming too old to take on such a burden as taking care of my mother. But I realized that we just live longer these days."

The important thing about this narrative scale is that it is not narrowly normative and fixed; it allows considerable diversity and flexibility. It is also "subjunctive," in the sense that it indicates how, starting from the "same place" at the "same time," one could come to be like this or like that—alternative lives that one might have chosen but did not. In short, the "Story of Our Class" provides the participants with a standardized catalogue of the possibilities and limitations for the classmate-cohort. It also provides a "timetable" (Roth 1963) that defines where you are in your lifecourse in comparison with others. And sometimes, the "Story of Our Class" contained in a reunion booklet becomes powerful reference material for self-examination and reorientation. Joan Miller relates how her fifteenth-year reunion and the reunion booklet affected her decision to divorce, brought out a sense of mortality, and reshaped her notion of the life cycle.

> I recall reading that booklet with a real sense of dismay, and thinking, "Is this really what I want?" I had always wanted to work, yet fifteen years after I graduated from high school, I had not done much with my life except that I was very involved in community organizations. And here were all those people who I had thought a lot dumber than I in high school were doing these wonderful things. I wasn't sure that going to that reunion was a very sensible thing. I think in some ways it led to the deterioration of my marriage.
>
> And then there were already some who had died. That was quite a shock to me. That's one thing that really fed a great deal into determining that I was going to do something for myself. Some died in Vietnam, some in freaky kinds of things, some died of heart attacks in their thirties. It was that sense of mortality that I didn't really feel before. And I think it probably reinforced my notion that if I was really going to do something with my life besides saying "someday," I'd better get on the stick, I didn't have forever.
>
> And I was not the only one who was in a sort of what we call a "midlife crisis." A lot of people in my class were changing jobs, getting divorces, or returning to school. TV and magazines talk about midlife crises as they occur in one's forties, but I think it actually happens earlier, in one's midthirties, when people start to think about their lives.

Every culture has a standard abstract version of the human life story (or stories) that involves a normative script and timetable, and against which we judge ourselves and others. The story of a reunion is more concrete and specific because it is based on the actual experiences of people whom one has known early in their—and one's own—lives. We use this story to correct the abstract and ideal cultural story, and thus produce a kind of "revised version" of the Bible of our own life. And this story, in turn, provides a provocative source of meaning by which we interpret our experiences. In short, the story becomes a guiding metaphor that influences and shapes the ways we construct our autobiographies.

We usually remember the realities of our past in our peripheral consciousness. In reunions these memories are refreshed and focused and even changed by the symbolic duality in the discourse. A high school reunion may be seen as a collective effort to give the past a place in participants' present lives. As Erikson (1968) pointed out, adolescence is the hardest stage of all to get through, among the eight transitional stages he identified, and the most influential in determining adult identity. But we cannot cling to this identity forever. We have to move on, go through changes. We have to weave meaning and identity out of additional episodes and experiences. In order to make this process more meaningful we go back to our symbolic roots—our high school experience being a powerful one—to find meaning and regain a sense of direction for the very act of making sense. In other words, in the reunion we look for a frame of significance for our emergent biography of the self with which to realign our lives to the future. In this sense the high school reunion is a ritual of a collective journey to the future as well. This is the intriguing paradox of reunions.

Reunion is different from cyclic "union" in which the same old story is told again and again. In each reunion there is a new story waiting for us, adding and accumulating meanings since our last moment of separation. As the Story of Our Class is enriched, so are our individual biographies.

3 Where the Hell Is Our Class President? Making Meaning Together

If anybody can answer this, we'll give you a chicken wing. Does anybody know the whereabouts of our class president, Bob Harris? He should be up here tonight doing this, instead of me. [A man in the audience shouts, "He's in jail!"] Jail? [laughter] Oh, no. We couldn't find him. Couldn't find a trace of him.

—*Master of Ceremonies, tenth-year reunion of Elm High Class of '72*

Talking with Americans, I find a paradox in the way they perceive reunions. On the one hand, high school reunions are generally regarded as a pan-American phenomenon. In trying to explain the reasons for having reunions to a Japanese observer, my informants emphasized the cultural and "traditional" rootedness of reunions in American society. High school reunions, said one, "like the Super Bowl or a Fourth of July parade, are more or less a tradition of this country." Some people even expressed puzzlement on finding out that I had been to many reunions for my project, since, as they see it, "reunions are similar any place you go." At the same time, most of the people I talked to never failed to stress that, despite the apparent similarities an ethnographer might find and that they themselves acknowledged, *their* reunion was unique. "You may have been to many reunions," I was told, "but ours would be something else." One man in the twentieth-year reunion of Elm High School congratulated me, saying, "You came to the right place. It's like hitting a jackpot. You'll find tonight what you have never found before, because our class is extraordinary." The apparent paradox in the comments people make about high school reunions attests to the existence of an incongruity between cultural perceptions and the feelings individuals have about their own reunions.

This incongruity is not difficult to understand. The high school reunion is a culturally recognized ritual frame that reproduces itself across the nation and across age groups, and the content within this ritual frame is culturally stylized. It is not surprising, therefore, that Americans tend to emphasize the cultural aspects of high school reunions when questioned by a foreign anthropologist. In the experience of each individual, however, a class reunion is not a cultural event but a personal one. He or she participates in a particular reunion as the bearer of a unique biography and memories about a specific high school experience. The people he or she comes to see at a reunion are not an abstract category of people bundled under the rubric "former classmates," but have concrete names and occupy certain special memories. The impetus for organizing and attending a reunion comes from the multiple specificities that a reunion provokes. This is why attending someone else's reunion—usually a spouse's—can be so boring.[1]

As a Japanese ethnographer interested in finding cultural processes and patterning, in Chapter 2 I adopted a synchronic perspective, taking a bird's-eye view and extrapolating the essential experiential features that characterize this American ritual. I did so in order to analyze the structure of the experience and the processes of storytelling and enactment that generate reflexivity and meaning. But while the synchronic view is heuristic in understanding the unique reflexive processes inherent in this cultural event, it obscures the array of creative activities invested by specific individuals in the construction of particular meanings, and does not explain why such meanings are important to those individuals.[2]

In this and subsequent chapters, therefore, I present concrete cases of high school reunions and explore the particular ways people experience reunions and construct meaning. First, I portray the tenth-year reunion of the Class of '72 from beginning to end, following the actions and discourse of participants from preparation to execution. My focus is on the collective construction of meaning, and on portraying the concrete ways in which two time consciousnesses shared by participants—historical and lifecourse—are enhanced and aligned in the creation of the Story of Our Class.[3]

Re-Membering the High School Class

The high school reunion is a voluntary activity. Each high school reunion is spontaneously initiated and hand-crafted by certain class members who volunteer to be program organizers. American public high schools do not provide institutional resources to tie alumni to their old schools or to support future class activities.[4] Nevertheless, Americans begin expressing vague but undeniable expectations of future reunions as early as the time of graduation. They also expect reunions to happen every five or ten years ("This year was the twentieth since I graduated, but I haven't heard anything about a reunion"). It is hard to render such anticipation into reality after the institutionally bounded high school community has been dissolved and members have taken to their separate paths. The timing of reunions therefore varies from one high school class to another. Some start their "reunion career" as early as the fifth year, while others never hold a reunion.

There are many objective factors that might influence the impetus for having a reunion, such as location or size of class, but in my own observations and in my interviews with Champaign-Urbana residents about their reunions, none of these emerged as definitive. Many interviewees suggested that the "closeness" of a class is the primary factor, but this folk theory is developed in retrospect, and it is hard to determine whether or not the perceived closeness really existed in high school or was formed by subsequent experiences at reunions.[5] In fact, the most crucial element in the materialization of any reunion is simply the willingness of class members still living in the high school community to become reunion organizers.

Although most Americans assume their class officers will continue to be in charge of organizing future class events, this expectation does not survive the test of time. In fact, among all the reunions I attended, there was only one case, the Elm High Class of '32, in which the Class President (and his wife, who had been Homecoming Queen) had consistently formed the nexus of every reunion committee. One informant told me her twentieth-year reunion was organized mainly by a group of former cheerleaders. Sometimes the committee for a subsequent reunion is appointed at the reunion itself, but committees established in this way are fragile; changes in appointees' lives that occur before the next reunion is held may prevent them from carrying out their roles. In most cases, the committee is established about a year before each reunion. Most typically, the idea for a class reunion is first conceived during a chance meeting of classmates, and the idea begins to take concrete shape only when these people become enthusiastic enough to become reunion organizers. Because of the spontaneous way in which reunions are initiated, many participants are surprised to find, contrary to their expectations, that the reunion committee is made up of a mixture of people who cannot be clearly characterized in terms of either their high school or their post–high school status.

What is more, each motley collection of self-appointed organizers must craft its particular reunion from scratch. Most have some idea of what a reunion should be like based on a hodgepodge of information gathered from other people's reunions stories and images of reunions in the mass media. But beyond this there is no cultural manual for reunions. There are no "ritual specialists," such as those who handle weddings or funerals, from whom to seek advice.[6] It is perhaps only natural, then, that organizers should tend to fall back on the very forms and skills they learned in high school through participating in such events as pep rallies, proms, assemblies, and class elections. This task of organizing a reunion requires imagination and creativity, since these "classic" forms must be applied to adults living under very different circumstances. This is especially true when, as in the case of the Class of '72, a reunion is to be the first since graduation.

STARTING A REUNION

John was thrilled when he heard the public service announcement on the radio while driving home from a baseball game in St. Louis one Sunday in June 1981: "Any member of the Class of '72 from Elm High School who would be interested in starting a reunion meeting, please contact Mary Walker." As soon as he got home, John called Betty, one of the few high school classmates he had kept in touch with through his college years and after.

John and Betty had been talking about starting a reunion themselves for almost a year at the time John heard the announcement. They had already discussed actual plans, such as selecting a restaurant for the event, making T-shirts to sell, and other possibilities that might make for a successful reunion. Whenever they met, they "fancied seeing those old familiar faces from high school," as Betty put it, whom they seldom if ever ran into in recent years. Their brainchild had been growing, but there was one thing John and Betty were not certain of: Would their high school classmates, who had been dubious about any organized activities in school, be interested in having a reunion? And, even if they were, how would they go about finding others who might cooperate to make their plans materialize?

When John and Betty were in high school, from 1969 to 1972, their school life was greatly affected by ferment over the Vietnam War, especially the student upheaval that struck the nearby university campus. The radical SDS (Students for a Democratic Society) dominated the Student Council, and a constant schism between Democrats and Republicans in school promoted students' awareness of political issues. Antiwar sentiment was widespread, as was fear of the draft. Traditional school events, such as proms or ball games, were staged against a backdrop of political debates and antiwar demonstrations. Also, more people in their class were planning to go to college than in any previous class. Until then, John told me, "the majority of the people started to work or got married right after graduation."

In John's mind, the memories of this high school atmosphere are still vivid:

> The people in our class were more or less the last people affected by the political upheaval. Our senior year was the last year, or next to the last year, of the draft, and some people actually did end up in Vietnam, though they came right back. You see, by the time they got there it was almost over, and they turned around and came back home. We also had a segment of the class that was pretty active in environmental issues and things like that. There were definitely political factions in high school. We had a segment of class members that were real SDS types—you know, "Let's blow something up." And at the other end we had those who were real archconservatives. I don't think that the percentages of people at the two extreme ends were that great, but they were pretty vocal. And then we had more or less the average people in the middle.

The political ferment of the time affected even "average people," including John. Although John himself "never really got to the point of demonstrating and marching a whole lot," he did read a lot of political materials and was actually in some of the demonstrations, as were many of his nonpolitical friends:

> I remember when I was a junior or sophomore, there was a big push for the eighteen-year-old vote, and I remember sitting on a committee that canvassed this part of the state for that. We went to various places in towns around this community, passing petitions and spending the weekends doing all sorts of things like that.
>
> To give you some idea of how we were then, our student government was not at all what you would imagine. Our Class President, for instance, was really a hell-raiser. He was the least of several evils. The way he got to be Class President was pretty weird, too. Keith Morgan ran against Bob. Keith was a rather serious, studious type (he's going to a law school now). He got up first on the stage and made a speech about all the good stuff he wanted to do for the class. Everybody yelled, "Sit down! Go away!" Bob got up after him and asked if everyone liked something. I don't remember what it was, but I am sure it was something really stupid. He then asked everyone to stand up if they liked it, and everyone did! We all laughed about the way everyone stood up, and when Bob said, "Vote for me," everyone yelled "All right!" and voted for him. It was just like that. That was exactly the kind of person everybody wanted.
>
> I remember one time our student government had a project. They were going to distribute Thanksgiving baskets to poor families the week before Thanksgiving. The baskets were all made up. The food was ready. The Class President was supposed to get the baskets and distribute them. Comes the day before Thanksgiving: "Bob, did you get the baskets?" He goes, "What for?" "Thanksgiving baskets." "Oh, uh, I have to go get the baskets!" So they gave him a pass out of school to go get the baskets and get them ready. There he was, on the night before Thanksgiving, driving to all those places like crazy: "Where do we go next? Where do we go next?" That was one of the many screw-ups we had.

John says this is why he and Betty felt they could not count on their class officers to take the initiative in organizing a reunion. "It was not just our Class President, but all of us. The whole school was just like that back in the sixties and early seventies. So we figured if we waited for the class officers to do it, it would never happen. Besides, we didn't know where they were. We couldn't even find our Class President."

So when John called Betty and told her about the reunion announcement, there was no debate; they instantly agreed they would join the reunion committee.

THE REUNION COMMITTEE

According to Mary Walker, the reunion was conceived accidentally when she ran into several classmates in a local restaurant one day: "When I started to talk to them, somebody mentioned that it's been ten years out of school. It came as a surprise to me because, though I think about high school a lot, the idea of its being ten years . . . ; it just didn't occur to me. And someone suggested a reunion and we all thought that would be great. So we decided to meet again to start planning." Mary and the others who initiated the reunion feel their class was "lucky to attempt to have a tenth reunion together," because when they were in school "it was just unpopular to do anything that had been popular in the past."

> Like we barely had a senior prom. There were only fifteen to twenty couples at the most. A lot of us were disappointed, but the class as a whole and the school as a whole didn't like those kinds of activities. I even thought at the time, "Gee, I wonder if we'll think we're missing a lot in later years when we look back and we haven't done all these dances you normally have—the homecoming dances and all that type of thing—and we'll be a little sorry." I kind of missed some of those things, but I'm sure most of them didn't. But *everyone* seems enthused about the reunion. I guess we are making up for what we've lost.

When John and Betty contacted Mary Walker in June, they found out that there had been one meeting of the organizing committee, but that not much had been decided except for the day of the reunion because, according to Mary, "the first meeting we spent laughing and talking." The date was set for Saturday, May 29, which would allow a year for locating former classmates and preparing for the event.

Between the initial idea of having a reunion and the actual materialization of the event lies a series of judgments and various levels of considerations that go into crafting a particular reunion event. The first pragmatic task the reunion organizers have to undertake is locating old classmates, mailing the invitations, and counting the number of people who plan to participate. This is challenging work, since most class members have lost touch with one another even in the relatively short period of ten years.

"The hardest part of the whole thing," Mary says, "was locating our classmates. We have a pretty large class—maybe the largest ever at Elm High. And people in our age group move around a lot." Just during the one-year preparation period, one committee member had a baby, two became pregnant (including Mary herself), and another moved out of town for a new job. This really made the committee members aware that "everybody is busy trying to be settled in adult society," as Mary put it. This lifecourse awareness was incorporated into the motto the committee members chose to print on the reunion invitation. The motto was taken from a song by Don McLean, a popular singer-songwriter, called "American Pie": *For ten years we've been on our own, but moss grows fat on a rolling stone.* "When John suggested this idea, we all thought it was neat," explains Mary. "The image of 'rolling stones' says a lot about what we are now."

The Class of '72 had 568 graduates. Because it was the first reunion since graduation, the committee thought they would start tracing classmates by contacting their former school. They were disappointed to find that the school kept no records of former students, and the school staff was too busy to help. They then decided to begin with a small booklet that had been published in the last month of their school days. First they typed names and last known addresses on index cards and arranged them in alphabetical order. Then they divided the cards among the committee members and started researching individual addresses, using the phone book and contacting parents, relatives, and friends who might know their classmates' whereabouts. At the second committee meeting, they traded cards so that a second person might fill in information the first could not locate. "It was really time-consuming work," says Mary. "But I was amazed that we got down to forty yet-to-be-located in the first couple of months. And since we started putting ads in the paper, we've gotten quite a few calls and have been able to locate even more of the original forty."

To her surprise, most of her classmates were still living in town or in satellite communities of Champaign-Urbana. "We've talked about it quite a lot in the committee meetings. It's very strange. All of us on the committee basically live in town, and yet we've scarcely seen each other since graduation. We can get lost even in this town."

The organizers had to make various decisions regarding the detailed arrangements for dinner, bands, decorations, and what kind of ceremonial events to stage. They explored various resources available to them, ascertaining the constraints of time and money, and also the talents, abilities, and degree of commitment each committee member could offer.

The committee had a total of seven meetings, all held at Mary's office, where she works as an interior designer. In the beginning, there were more than fifteen people, but attendance fluctuated, and by early March, three months before the event, the nucleus of the committee came to consist of five women and two men. This unstable attendance of committee members was also a reflection of the current life situations of former classmates. As Mary said, "We honestly have no time. I know in my parents' reunions a whole bunch of the women worked on the committee who didn't work, but there isn't anyone on our committee that doesn't have a full-time job. So it's really hard to fit meetings into your schedule, and some of us even don't have regular schedules, like from eight to five." So, instead of burdening committee members with too much work and expecting their total devotion, they had to organize the event in the most labor-efficient way and with minimum expense. As Mary explains, "We just wanted to do as much as we knew we could handle and do it well, and that didn't include a lot of extras. Besides, we didn't have money. So we fifteen [who gathered for the first meeting] paid in advance to raise money for the mailing of the reunion announcements."

Although time and money were limited, each committee member had a specialty to contribute. Betty, a nutritionist, offered her expertise in planning meals for the reunion dinner and for the picnic the next day. Kathy, a secretary at a dentist's office, offered to do the mailing. John, a music buff who works at a printing company, took care of printing souvenir T-shirts and selecting a band. Janis, who had access to a copy machine, made all the name tags with reproductions of senior pictures from the yearbook. Mary, in addition to providing a meeting place and being the contact person for former classmates, designed decorations for the reunion site. David, a former "class clown" who now manages a department store, contributed his sense of humor and smooth-talking skills by serving as Master of Ceremonies and collecting humorous gifts for the awards ceremony.

Operating side by side with pragmatic tasks for organizing a reunion are the interpretative actions of making the gathering of high school classmates meaningful in their present lives. This is, in its essence, a process of "re-membering" the past high school community. In this case, re-membering means the reaggregation of the cast of characters in the Story of Our Class with their own prior selves—the significant images of themselves and others without which the story could not be written. In planning the concrete agenda for the event, the organizers continually looked back at what their classmates were like in school and speculated on what they might be like now, in order to "satisfy the majority of the people," as Mary put it. "We had so many different types of people in our class. We tried to remember what they liked and didn't like, although we kept telling ourselves at the same time that maybe they would not be the same people we remember from ten years ago."

The unexpectedly heated debate concerning which music to play was an acute reminder that although they share a "flower children" past, they had since become very different kinds of people. Mary soon realized that even the committee was composed of people with different ideas and lifestyles when they started to debate so intensely about what kind of band to hire. The conflict was between those who supported nostalgic rock 'n' roll from the sixties and seventies, and those who insisted on something up-to-date. Mary explains: "I personally wanted to have a disc jockey and play the songs which were popular when we were in high school, but some other people felt very strongly that they didn't want to look back, but wanted to look ahead. Finally I said 'fine' because it wasn't worth arguing about. But this whole discussion made me aware of what different lifestyles and viewpoints we all have now."

In the process of preparation, the past is evoked and the present imagined, and, in the fashioning of the event, both are juxtaposed in the way most fitting to their image of the class. Here are some examples.

The organizers decided to reprint senior pictures from their high school yearbook on nametags, because these pictures captured the images they projected in high school as "flower children." "It looks more drastic to me now when I look at my yearbook," said Mary. "We all had the perfect look of 'flower children.' I don't want to say hippie or anything else. Yeah, 'flower children.'" But Mary and the other committee members were aware that some people might not like to be reminded of how they looked in high school: "We thought it would be funny. We all had such long hair, really long. . . . Most of the girls had straight hair, like Joan Baez. Even those people who I thought were conservative had super-long hair, too. It was everyone, no matter what their political views were. It was just the way things were then."

The organizers decided to give awards in order to evoke a high school atmosphere, as well as to call attention to where they were ten years after graduation. They decided against publishing a reunion booklet, however, though they knew it to be a "typical thing to do for our parents' reunions," because they imagined that their classmates were mobile people. It was too early to fix their lives on a printed page. In Mary's words:

> We figured that we don't have that much to say in ten years after graduation, and we will change addresses and jobs anyway in the next five or ten years, by the time we have another reunion. Besides, there will be enough of who's got the best job, who's doing this and who's doing that at the reunion anyway 'cause everybody's gonna ask everybody. But we didn't want to print it in a book. We said that maybe by the fifteenth or twentieth reunion, we might want to distribute booklets containing all that information, but we sure didn't want it after ten years and decided unanimously that we would not ask them anything else except to come.

In fact, finding a practical way to get "independent-minded" people together was the hardest task of all. "We thought if we asked them to do this or that, they would go, 'Wait a minute!' That would be way too much for them. We were just that way." One example is the way people made their reservations:

> We'd asked them to send in reservations by March, but we found that that was a mistake. People just didn't care about the due date. So we sent a second mailing to remind them. So far I've gotten close to 200 reservations, but even now I hear from many people that so-and-so is coming, and I don't have reservations for them. I know that they will just show up at the door.

Predicting the unpredictability of their classmates, the committee selected a buffet-style dinner for the reunion in order to accommodate their old "flower children" selves, who valued individual freedom and flexibility over structured, imposed choices and diversity over uniformity, as well as their present "rolling stone" selves, whose unstable life situations might prevent them from making plans in advance. In this way they could cope with last-minute attendees as well as the presumed diversity of tastes in food. The committee also made sure the food for the next day's picnic would be catered, to relieve the women from the burden of preparing lunch. Mary says, "You know, most of the women in our class work, and they're not into cooking too much. If we ask them to fix all those dishes, they probably won't come. We had to make all possible efforts to make this reunion an all-you-have-to-do-is-show-up type of thing, which fits right into our class image."

The reunion T-shirt the committee decided to sell to raise money for the picnic and possibly for a future reunion was the result of a "brainstorm" that Betty had even before the committee was formed. "I saw kids wearing T-shirts with the name of the high school class and all the names of graduates when I was working at the university cafeteria. When I saw them I thought, 'Gee, why doesn't our class do something like that at our tenth reunion?' So I suggested the idea and everyone liked it." The T-shirt was in their school colors (red with black print), with a cardinal on front and their graduation program and the names of all the classmates printed on the back. The design of the T-shirt symbolically reestablishes the group's membership. Moreover, as a "shared asset of the class" that would bind them to future reunions, the T-shirt sale reiterated the sense of solidarity necessary for creating a "reunion tradition." In short, the sale of the reunion T-shirt is a symbolic reconfirmation of the past high school community as well as of the promise to hold future reunions.

Re-Encountering

ANTICIPATION

On May 21, the committee gathered for a last-minute check-up. One hundred and seventy-eight reservations had been made, one-third of them by people living out of town. One classmate was coming from Alaska, another from California, and many from Chicago. Everyone on the committee looked relaxed, knowing that everything was set for the event.

"So the committee will sit at the reception table and distribute nametags as people come in, right? Should we check receipts?" Kathy asked.

"Oh, sure. Because there are some guys who are good at sneaking in and out," John joked, recalling the high school "jerks" (his word) who used to escape from school meetings to hang out in the park.

BETTY: Are those people coming? I bet not.

JOHN: Who knows? We can't judge from the names on the reservations.

KATHY: Do you think we can recognize people? It would be embarrassing if we couldn't remember names when they come to the reservation desk.

DAVID: I don't think we change that much in ten years. Besides, we had five hundred or so students in our class. We can't remember them all anyway.

JOHN: By the way, why don't those people who are still in town come?

KATHY: I saw Joyce Miller, you know her; she was a cheerleader in our junior year, but later became politically active and—

JOHN: Oh, yeah, I remember her. She was in my Spanish class.

KATHY: She said she can't make it because her husband is going on a business trip to California and she's going with him.

BETTY: Is she married? Oh, my God! Wasn't she one of those feminists who were pretty vocal about pursuing a career and not getting married?

JOHN: I don't remember her in particular, but there were a lot of girls like her.

DAVID: Bill said he saw Richard Smith the other day. Bill asked him if he was planning on coming to the reunion, and Richard said "I'm not interested." Just like that. Period. What kind of a joke is that?

MARY: I received many nice regret letters, too. Dorothy Williams said that she just had a baby and it's too much for her to make the trip from Ohio. And there was another one from St. Louis. What was his name? Oh, yeah, Steve MacCauley. Says he's just started a new job and is too busy to come. And Susan Ross—it was kind of funny—said she can't come because her father's wedding is on the same day.

JANIS: Remember Bill Tucker? He wrote me a letter. So I wrote him back. He's going to a business school.

JOHN: Bill in business school?

JANIS: Yeah, it's a shame he's not going to come to the reunion, because we could discuss Reaganomics. That ought to send him for a—

JOHN: Oh, I could see it. Bill, he'd send us a letter back saying, [imitating Bill] "Due to current economic trends, I will not be attending . . ."

JANIS: He probably ripped that letter in half, 'cause he and I used to argue constantly . . .

DAVID: What was he? Total communist?

JANIS: You know, Democrat, real liberal. I mean *real* liberal. Of course, I was completely obnoxious. That's why we used to argue.

MARY: Yeah, he was a great liberal.

JANIS: He was, wasn't he? I liked him really well, though.

DAVID: He was the only football player that won that
          moratorium. He got kicked off the team because he was
          involved in politics.

JOHN: Oh, yeah, I completely forgot about that!

DAVID: They were gonna kick him off, and then they said they
          couldn't do it because—

JOHN: Smike went, [imitating the coach's voice] "I ain't having
          no communist on my team. I ain't having it!!!"

BETTY: Where's our Class President anyway? No one knows?

DAVID: Nope! But it's strange. Apparently, his parents moved
          away a long time ago and nobody knows anything about
          him at all.

JANIS: How about teachers? Are they coming?

MARY: We couldn't find some of them, but I invited the ones
          we could get hold of. They said they would come, but
          now I'm not sure.

JOHN: Can you believe that we're older now than many of
          those teachers were when we were in school?

JANIS: They were like twenty-three or twenty-four, weren't they?

KATHY: Are we going to sit together at one table?

JOHN: No. I think it would be better if we mingle.

MARY: I agree. We want to make sure that everyone feels
          welcome. We'd better take the initiative to talk to as
          many people as we can.

KATHY: But don't give me the evil eye if I just talk to my friends.

After the committee members hurried back to their homes or to
night jobs, Mary stayed for a while to clean up and talked to me about
her expectations. Most of all, she was concerned about everyone feeling
welcome and thinking the reunion was worthwhile, because, although
Mary herself enjoyed her high school days, she knew there are those
who feel bitter about their high school experience:

A few had said—and I can believe this—that high school was the
worst years of their lives, and they sure don't want to return and talk

about it. It's a real time of upheaval in your life anyway. I mean, everything was such a big deal. If your face breaks out, it seems like it's the
end of the world. You never want to make a fool of yourself in front of
people, and never want to say the wrong thing, and everything was
such a big deal then. It wasn't the happiest time in a lot of people's
lives, I'm sure. And I don't think I want to go back to that period of
life again, though I had a pretty easy time of it. So I can understand
some people not wanting to come back. Some, I'm sure, feel bitter.

To her surprise, however, "judging from the names who made reservations, every type of person is coming." Not just "the ones who run
around with those who run around," but those who kept low profiles in
high school as well. "I have to tell you this. The guy who had the
longest hair—curled down almost to his waist—was one of the first to
make a reservation. Isn't it something?"

"But what made people decide to come?" I asked. After thinking a
while, Mary decided that curiosity was the primary reason. At least in
her case, "I come out of nothing else but curiosity." She continued:

Even if I didn't want to see friends and talk about things we used to
do, I would come for curiosity's sake. I'm interested in seeing how
they look because we all looked so distinctive in high school. People
at the meeting haven't changed so much, other than, of course, that
they've changed their hairstyle, they've grown up, and they're a lot
more mature—I hope, anyway. But our committee's so small, so it's
hard to compare it to the whole class.

This friend of mine—we were best friends in high school—called
me from Ohio a couple of nights ago and she said, "Won't it be fun
to see who looks different and who doesn't?" And I said, "Yeah, I
heard that men go to pot and the women look the same at the ten-
year reunion." We're interested to see if that's true or not.

In addition to satisfying her curiosity about how her classmates have
changed, Mary was also curious to see if the clear boundaries that
existed between the different social groupings in high school would still
be in place:

You know, in high school there were definite cliques. And I like to
think that I wasn't in any of them, because I really wasn't. I did go

to games but I also didn't hang around with the cheerleaders, or . . . You know, I just wasn't in any of them. I have a group of friends that really didn't care one way or the other as far as that goes. But there were definite cliques at the time. I guess we always have them, but in high school it was quite obvious. I'm curious to see how they would act toward each other.

She predicted that "people would be pretty mellow." Not only that they have grown to be "more adult" and able to deal with various different types of people, but also, Mary emphasized, that they would now share "common ground" by virtue of the fact that those who come to the reunion are the ones who find meaning in seeing and talking to former classmates:

> Even if they weren't in the same clique or didn't talk to each other in high school, I bet everybody talks to everyone and acts like they were long-lost friends. I know I would talk to people that I didn't know very well then. Not necessarily because I did or didn't like them, but just because now we have a common ground more than we did then, since we all bothered to come. So you have something to talk about—at least ask them what they're doing and that type of thing. This is why a lot of us [on the committee] were saying today that we don't want to sit with the people on the committee, because we've gotten to know each other again and we want to meet other people and talk to them and to mix with people all night long, not just hang out in little groups. We'll see if that works.

THE REUNION

Saturday, May 29, and the tenth-year reunion of Elm High School's Class of '72 is blessed with beautiful spring weather. "Perfect weather to dress any way you like," Mary says. Betty has arranged everything through a four-star restaurant in a small mall on the edge of town.

The committee members have been here since five P.M., two hours before the reception is to begin. Tables and chairs are laid out in the empty mall, which is closed for the day, waiting to be filled by old friends—and enemies—most of whom have not seen one another for ten years.

John and Betty are setting up the reception desk. In front of them,

Kathy is trying to fix a board to the wall that will be covered with letters from people who could not attend. One of the letters begins, "Since I can't be with you today, I thought I'd at least let you know what I've been doing the last ten years." Most of the letters give a short summary of the writer's life after high school. One letter is from Canada, from a classmate whose name had been on the committee's missing-persons list. Another is from a woman in California, who regrets that she cannot come because she is expecting a baby. A letter from Bangkok, Thailand, contains the long life story of a classmate who started out as a dental hygiene specialist, went to Hawaii and Cambodia with Youth with a Mission, and ended up as a missionary in Bangkok. Some have sent pictures of themselves with their spouses and children. Without exception, the letters ask for any reunion publication, pictures, or other memorabilia through which the writers can feel some connection to their high school class.

Mary is checking to see that all the tables are decorated as she had requested. Each table was supposed to be covered with a floor-length linen cloth and have a bouquet of red and white flowers with a little cardinal stuck in it. "Actually," Mary says to a man from the restaurant who has come to help with the preparations, "our school colors were red and black, but who wants black flowers?" Mary then goes from one table to another, placing a reunion program on each plate. The program is bright red with black letters that read:

Elm High Class of 1972: Ten Year Reunion Dinner-Dance

SATURDAY, MAY 29, 1982

Reception 6:00 P.M.–7:00 P.M.

Cocktail Hour 7:00 P.M.–8:00 P.M.

Dinner 8:00 P.M.–8:30 P.M.

Awards and Recognition of Committee 8:30 P.M.–9:30 P.M.

Visiting Time 9:30 P.M.–1:00 A.M. Band Plays

The frame for the reunion has been carefully crafted by the reunion committee, but they expect that what actually will happen in the reunion is beyond their ability to predict. Venturing into the realm of unpredictability is the essence of what draws former schoolmates back together. They do not know how much their classmates have changed ("Will I recognize them?"), and they do not know how changes in their own lives might appear to classmates ("Will they recognize me?"). Participating in a reunion is a kind of "thrill-seeking behavior" (Scheff 1979: 13); if they knew the answers to all these questions, there would be no point in attending the reunion. The committee members look tense; the enthusiasm they showed at the last meeting has faded into an anticipation that is almost dread. They seldom joke or laugh. Some even look depressed.

"Oh my God, they're starting to come," Betty whispers at the reception desk.

"Take it easy," John replies.

First, a group of four women arrive. They mention their names and, one by one, pick up their nametags and quietly proceed to the cocktail lounge.

"I didn't recognize any of them. Did you?" Betty asks John.

"Me neither," John answers. "If I didn't know them in school, why would I know them now?"

A line of participants starts to form in front of the reception desk around six o'clock. The waiting line looks like the clothing section of a mail-order catalogue in terms of the variety of styles. Most of the women are in one-piece dresses, ranging from expressionless polyester to well-tailored party dresses. There are no women dressed in blue jeans, however—the popular attire of their high school days. The men's dress is more diverse, including three-piece suits, sporty pants and shirts, blue jeans with T-shirts, and earth-colored work clothes with a company name printed on the chest pocket.

The atmosphere at the gateway to yesteryear is rather low-key at first; there is none of the hugging and kissing typical at the receptions of older people's reunions (see Chapter 5). But gradually the initial tension is relieved somewhat as they start a guessing game with newcomers and exchange jokes about the senior-year pictures printed on the nametags.

"Guess who?" A man wearing a cowboy hat steps up to the reception desk.

"Wait a minute! Don't say it yet! I know who you are . . ."

Betty searches her memory.

"Keith Barnes!" a woman farther back in line guesses correctly, and receives a cheer. "Last week, when I had free time at work, I looked through the yearbook to brush up on faces," she admits.

"Ah, no. Good-bye." The next woman pretends to walk away as soon as she notices the senior pictures on the nametags, neatly laid out on the reception desk.

"Hey, Dan, you wanna see my high school senior picture?" she asks as she turns to her date standing a couple of steps apart from the crowd.

"I know you." Mary points at a man with a neat crew-cut who is next in line. "Well, but I can't remember . . ."

As Mary ponders, the man pulls out his driver's license and shows her his picture, saying, "This may be closer to the way I looked in high school."

"Oh, Matt Baker!"

The guessing games improvised by the reuniters serves as an icebreaker and relieves some of the anxiety of dealing with old friends who appear in the guise of adult strangers.

Dinner is served a little before eight. By this time, the committee members have scattered to be with friends. The reunion site is now filled with the sound of conversation. Old friendships—and a few flames—are rekindled, and stories of what people have been doing during the last ten years are exchanged. Some people move from one table to another, trying not to miss any of the particular friends they have come to see.

At one table, the conversation is dominated by the story of the "wonderful little family" of Trudy, an ex-cheerleader who is now a mother of two. The main listener is Vicki, a fellow ex-cheerleader who is unmarried and is working in a corporate attorney's office:

VICKI: I want to see your kids.

TRUDY: I'm bringing them to the picnic tomorrow.

VICKI: I'll bet you make an excellent mother.

TRUDY'S HUSBAND:
      She can be violent.

TRUDY:
      Yeah, "Clean your room! Be quiet! Brush your teeth!"
      That's basically what you hear. My loud voice helped
      me to lead cheers, but it helps me to be a mother,
      too.

VICKI:
      Are you planning to have another one soon?

TRUDY:
      Um, he says "no."

VICKI:
      Oh, two is no fun.

TRUDY'S HUSBAND:
      I haven't made up my mind for certain yet, but at
      this point, two is plenty.

VICKI:
      I'd like to have one myself, but I don't know if I'll
      ever find time to be married, let alone have a kid. I
      would have loved to see you pregnant, Trudy.

TRUDY:
      Oh, I looked like a keg! [she laughs]

Apparently the smooth social interaction between Vicki and Trudy is imbued with a personal history unknown to the outside observer. One woman at the same table will give me her interpretation of this interaction later: "I was amazed that they were still competing with each other after all those years. They were sort of rivals, you know. Now they have completely different lifestyles but are still trying to impress each other: 'I am a perfect mom' and 'I am a career woman.' It was absurd."

Meeting old friends means meeting your old self. Each meeting brings back remembered images of high school selves, and tends to develop into a minidrama. There must be dozens of little dramas that I am unaware of being played out around these tables. John will tell me about one of these the next day:

I wouldn't be surprised if one or two couples rekindled old flames in the reunion and would be married by the time of our fifteenth reunion. Like Bruce and Vicki. Do you remember a couple who was dancing from the beginning to the end? There were a couple of other ones, but they would be top of the list! Vicki Lewis was a Homecoming Queen. And she was Bruce's heartthrob in high school. Bruce knew that Vicki dated Tom, a football player, but didn't know to what extent. We figured that it might be better if we just kept it that way. Actually, it was more serious than that. Well, going through the line (to get food at the reunion buffet), Bruce got ahead of me and he looked back and there was Vicki. He goes, "Hey, John, is that Vicki?" I heard that later in the evening Bruce went up to Tom and said, "Tom, it's good to see you are the same overbearing son-of-a-bitch you always were." And Tom just sort of smiled and walked off. I thought it was a real good shot. You'd not know what I mean unless you had known Tom in high school.

And yet, there are some faces people cannot remember from high school. At some of the tables people are hunched together, examining their senior yearbook to find pictures of those they cannot recognize. "Here he is. Now I know who he is," says one woman. The senior pictures in the high school yearbook are visual testimony about high school selves and symbols of membership in the class. Unless a person is located and recaptured in the frozen image in the yearbook, anyone who was not close to that person cannot gain the sense of knowing him or her and cannot re-establish their relationship.

The dramas of re-encountering spark a variety of reflexive moments in the minds of the individual participants. I will discuss this fully in the next chapter, but for now, my story moves to the ceremonial events and the collective rewriting of the Story of Our Class.

Rewriting

"Can the people on the south side hear me?" the Master of Ceremonies asks of the people sitting around the tables at the farthest edge of the shopping mall. "People on the south side, if you want to win a prize come on down so you can hear me." On the stage, the Awards Ceremony is beginning. Eight reunion awards are to be granted in the relaxed after-dinner atmosphere. The eight awards chosen by the organizers include: The Most Children, The Least Changed, The Most Changed, The Grayest, The Most Eligible Man, The Most Eligible

Woman, Came the Farthest, and New Class Clown. The ceremony proceeds from one award to another, and the adult selves that these former high school students have become over the last ten years are literally put on the stage, providing participants an opportunity to collectively assess changes and continuities, and to examine the meaning of the last ten years for the members of the Class of '72.

The first award to be granted is Most Children. "Now who has the most children?" The M.C. looks for candidates. "Three. All right, I want to know who has at least four kids right now. Four kids? Nobody? All right, you've got three kids. Stacy has three kids. Wait a minute; Jose has three, too."

A woman at my table looks surprised. "Four kids!? How could that be possible? When did they get married?" "I don't know. I know Stacy was married the year after we were graduated," another replies. They count the years to estimate the timing of childbirth. "Well, actually it does make sense, doesn't it? But is there anyone who has four kids?"

It turns out that no one has four children.

Okay, Stacy came up with a tie breaker. How old's your oldest child? Seven, all right. How old is yours? Seven and a half, all right. Okay, here's the tie-breaker. Stacy's is seven, and Colleen's is seven and a half. We're going to have to get down to months and days. Who else has three? Come on. How old's your oldest child? Six? All right you're out of it. [audience laughs] How old are your children, Megan? Eleven? [applause] You got three? All right, we got a new winner. You just hold tight [laughter]. Or do your best to hold tight.

"All right, Megan, you come up here. Bring your hubby, too." The M.C. confers the prize he has chosen for this special couple: "A home-made, do-it-yourself vasectomy kit"—complete with surgical gloves and mask, a razor ("We gotta prep your husband for this"), scissors, merthiolate (to prevent infection), smelling salts, and, in lieu of anesthesia, a silver bullet to bite down on. The audience laughs and applauds as he explains the use of the prize, but the couple is obviously embarrassed.

Whenever you're ready to quit having children—You are? Then go home tonight and use this. Even if you decide not to do the procedure, the kit includes a ten-day-guaranteed option. You don't need the mask, the razor, the merthiolate, the smelling salts, or the bullet. All you need is the gloves and the scissors; that should give you a ten-day supply of . . . well, never mind [the audience roars with laughter]. I'll give you the instructions later.

. . .

Now we're going to get into the person who came the farthest. Steve came all the way from Alaska. Unless somebody came in from overseas . . . I don't think nobody's gonna top Steve, right? Come on down Steve. I donated this personally. It's a road atlas [someone yells, "All right!"]. Everybody give Steve a hand [applause].

Other awards are decided by taking nominations from the floor.

"Okay, The Least Changed. We've got somebody in mind, but I'll tell you what: Anybody who wants to, we'll give you about five seconds to come up with some nominations. Now, you can pick anyone you know who hasn't changed a bit."

"Hasn't changed a bit? That's impossible," says Lorraine at her table.

"Trudy, number one nomination. Ron Gould, number two. Larry Edwards, number three. Everybody that was nominated come up here. Ann Peters. All right, Jim Turner. Hurry up Jim, come on up. I want to start taking a vote. Come on Jim. Larry, come on. Michelle? Oh yeah, she hasn't changed. Come on Michelle."

Someone yells, "Tom Wolf! He's still drunk!"

"Tom Wolf? Oh yeah, personality-wise hasn't changed. Come on, Tom . . .

"All right, let's close the nominations, we've got to move on. All right, everybody stand in line. Okay, number one: Trudy Williams? If you approve, clap."

The crowd cheers for Trudy.

"Number two: Ann Peters."

Silence. The crowd laughs.

"This is Ann Peters. See, nobody recognized you, Ann. Ann, you're out [more laughs]. All right: Michelle Gateman [scattered applause]. Diana Gates [someone yells 'Yeah!']. Is that it? George Miller."

A group of women cheers enthusiastically. Lorraine says, "I like George Miller's groupies."

Another woman at the table says, "I don't know who George Miller is."

Trudy is voted Least Changed. As the award is presented, a former classmate at my table comments cynically, "She hasn't changed a bit. Not only in the way she looks, but also in the way she brags about herself."

"Now we're going to have the *Most* Changed. How 'bout a nomination? Mark Stevens? Mark, come on. Now you won't recognize him when you see him." As other nominees are presented, the audience "oohs" and "aahs" in disbelief. One woman at the table can't place one of the nominees: "Who is that person there in the yellow short-sleeved shirt? Who is that? How can I vote for him if I can't remember who he is?"

"Line up, line up," the M.C. urges. "Look at all these Young Republicans up here. Mike Corbaccio? Where's he?"

"Oh yeah," says Lorraine, "Mike's a good one."

Another woman at our table agrees: "Corbaccio is unbelievable."

Mike Corbaccio, as John will tell me later, used to be a student activist and "the consummate hippie of the class."

As Mike approaches the stage in clean-cut hair and a conservative dark suit and tie, the M.C. says, "Oh my gosh." The crowd cheers. Mike wins the Most Changed award easily.

"Okay, let's move along." The M.C. continues the ceremony. "Most Eligible Man. All right, let's get this one. Who's single? Ron Lewis, come on up here. Ken Gross, come on up here. How 'bout all the single men coming up here? All the single men, you wanna come up here? Get Ron Lewis up here, he's pretty eligible." The men line up on stage. "All right. Now, ladies vote only. Let's play a little dating game here."

The women at my table discuss the nominees. "Chris Who? Oh, yeah. I'll vote for him; but, boy, he's changed."

The women choose a future doctor, Glen, over a handsome musician by a narrow margin. As the M.C. presents the winner, he says, "Hey, Glen here looks a little bit like Joe Namath, doesn't he?"

"Okay, now it's the girls' turn." One of the men in the audience shouts, "All right!"

"Come on, single girls." The Most Eligible Woman award is met with resistance. No one approaches the stage. The M.C. now has to modify the spirit of this award. "All right, who's single but don't want to be married?"

A woman shouts, "Yeah!" Another says, "Right here!"

"Come on up here."

"No way!"

"Come on. I've got to have some people up here. They won't come up. Will all the single women come up? Nice to see the big turn-out here."

"They've all gotten married," suggests one of the women.

"Come on," pleads the M.C.

"Chickens!" shouts one of the men.

"Don't you want to get married?" another man asked from the floor. A woman from the floor shouts, "No-o-o!"

"Why?"

"I want to fool around!"

A few women reluctantly move to the stage as the men begin to coax individual women. "Now, who doesn't want to get married?" the M.C. asks again.

A woman raises her hand and reads aloud a list of grievances from a book called *Why Men Have to Win*:

> They never put the toilet seat down.
> They're impossible to shop for.
> They treat sex as a game.
> They always come first.

After the defiantly single women have been given their forum, the selection continues.

"Okay, men vote for this: Most Eligible . . ." He turns to the few brave women who have come forward. "You think this might be embarrassing?"

"Yes!"

Another woman says she doesn't mind.

"Okay, we're gonna have a vote. If you mind, you can sit down. It'll be fun, don't worry about it."

One woman in particular attracts attention. Her tight, short skirt and frilly blouse set off her slender figure to its full advantage, and her cutting-edge hairstyle makes her look like a cover girl from *Cosmopolitan*.

"Who is she?" people at my table whisper to one another.

"I've been wondering who that girl is ever since I walked in here, but can't remember. You know, she was sitting at the table with Rick Keller."

"Oh, yeah, she's gorgeous! Who is she?"

"I can't find her in the yearbook. Did we have someone like her in our class?"

"I don't know. It's hard to remember without seeing her [senior] picture."

The "cover girl" is voted Most Eligible Woman unanimously.

The M.C. presents the next award, the Grayest. He explains that the committee thought of giving the Baldest, too, but decided not to because "that's kind of crude." "All right. I don't think we have to vote on the next one." "Bob!" shouts out a woman at my table, and the audience cheers in agreement. "Okay, it's Doctor Zhivago's double, here." The crowd laughs. "I don't think nobody would want to challenge that." Bob's prize is a bottle of Grecian Formula 44 with Ronald Reagan's picture pasted on the front.

In the selection of New Class Clown, the kind of skit participants became familiar with in high school is recreated.

"All right, we're taking nominations for a New Class Clown now. Tim Murphy? Okay, Tim, come on up. Any more nominations?"

A woman yells, "Donahue!"

"Ned Donahue. Any more? Dan Keifer . . ."

"I think the best way to determine this is to have everyone do a minute skit."

The crowd applauds in approval. "And whoever gets the most applause will be the New Class Clown, 1982. You'll serve the term until our, well, our fifteenth, twentieth . . . until we hold the next one. So get your best together, boys. Just say something."

The first nominee steps up to the mike, and the woman who nominated him yells, "Say something intelligent, Donahue!"

"I'd like to thank everybody for coming out tonight, and my producer and director, and, of course, Mom and Dad, for making this all possible." This falls flat with the crowd, as does the next contestant's attempt.

Finally, Tim Murphy steps up to the mike and brings down the house by simply saying, "The lettuce was limp," referring (to the embarrassment of the management) to the lifeless salad that had come with the meal.

Apparently, Tim's non sequitur evokes the memory of their Class President who won office in a similar way. After naming Tim Murphy the New Class Clown, the M.C. confers for a moment with a classmate, then steps back up to the mike.

"Larry Edwards just came up with a very interesting present," he announces, and offers a chicken wing to anyone with information about the missing Class President. "We couldn't find him. Couldn't find a trace of him. We just thought somebody might have some inside information they could share with us." No one wins this prize.

The mystery of the whereabouts of the Class President inspires speculation and jokes that will carry over to the next day's picnic. The missing President becomes the unseen protagonist of the reunion discourse. In exchanging their ideas of what might have happened to him in the last ten years, participants relate their own life situations. But one feeling expressed by many in the process of speculation is that perhaps he is just like one of them, experimenting with his life somewhere, "trying to make it" in adult society.

At the conclusion of the ceremonies, the M.C. honors each committee member, calling attention to the contributions each has made toward the evening's success. "But most of all, I want to thank you, because this was a very successful reunion. We were dreaming of 200, and it looks like we got about 220." He then makes some announcements regarding the picnic, the availability of T-shirts, and details on who to contact about helping with the fifteenth-year reunion. "In the next reunion, we'll make sure to put Bob [the missing President] on the stage and make him explain his mysterious disappearance. All right. The band will play until 1:00. Don't get too rowdy."

By re-membering the old high school class, the reunion confronts participants with new "realities" generated in the ten years since graduation. We have seen in the case of the tenth-year reunion of the Elm High School Class of '72 a discursive process in which participants gradually discard the old stories of themselves from high school and create new stories of their lives. Their awareness of their position in history and lifecourse is enhanced and given symbolic expression through such "summarizing symbols" (Ortner 1973) as "flower children" and "rolling stones."

The "missing President" personifies the idealized life-narrative of the Class of '72, in that he has become (or so they imagine) what they once predicted they would be like ten years after graduation. Many members of the Class of '72 believed during high school that free-spirited flower children with a rebellious view of the establishment would never "give a damn" (John's words) about something like a class reunion. In the discourse about his whereabouts, the Class President provoked nostalgia over what they had been like and what they had thought they might become, and in the process he became a "model" by which participants could gauge their own lives, as well as a catalyst for understanding their collective experience as former flower children busily trying to establish themselves in adult society. In this way, the Class President re-established himself as the "hero" of the revised edition of the Story of Our Class.

The award-giving ceremony was a performance of this revision. By seeking out those members whose lives seemed to have progressed further than others', and comparing how they are now and how they were then, the award-giving ceremony attempts to fix the meaning of the past ten years. Ten years could take Steve as far as Alaska geographically, and Bob to a gray head biologically. A few women have three children, and many others are still unmarried. And the resistance demonstrated by some women to the Most Eligible Woman award is an indication of the new mores and lifestyles these early 1970's graduates are creating. Ten years did not affect Trudy's appearance or personality much, though she is married and has become a mother. And yet ten years can transform "flower children" into "Young Republicans"—and can make a former student activist feel comfortable in a conservative dark suit and tie.

The Story of Our Class is prospective as well as retrospective, creating a vision of the future while at the same time looking back on the past. It also creates a new bonding among participants by providing a common meaning they will draw on to make sense of their lives. The first reunion is a stepping-stone toward the transformation of a high school class into a community of meaning. The selection of the New Class Clown may be indicative of the hope of members to maintain the continuity of this community by preserving the class's "traditional" sense of humor.

The Story of Our Class constructed in this reunion will remain intact until the next reunion, when it will be revised again. Will the Class President, as promised, be the M.C. of that reunion?

Good to See You: Reunions and Biographical Processes

Most of us don't want to be who we were in high school, and assure
ourselves we're not. But all alone, in the middle of the night, we
sometimes wonder, what would it be like if I went back to high
school today? Would anything have changed? Would I?

—*Ralph Keyes,* Is There Life After High School?

In the previous chapter, we saw the ways in which collective meaning
was constructed in the tenth-year reunion of the Class of '72. The Story
of Our Class that emerged in the reunion is a symbolic articulation of
collective experience, and provides a frame of significance by which
members of the class can interpret their own lives. Through the construction of collective meaning, the high school reunion works to har-
monize individual experience and consciousness, but the reunion experiences of individuals are never homogeneous. Participants each
experience a reunion differently and interpret their experiences from
the vantage point of their own biographical perspective. Oftentimes,
people go to a reunion with a specific goal in mind.

In this chapter, I focus on individual action and experience. I have
chosen two individuals from the Class of '72, John and Betty, both of
whom served on the reunion committee. As we have already seen, both
John and Betty are reunion enthusiasts. They had been eagerly anticipating a reunion for some time, and joined the reunion committee as
soon as they heard the announcement. In my meetings with them, they
mentioned more than once that they joined the reunion committee
simply because they had both become nostalgic about high school over

the past few years and wanted to see "those kids" they went to high school with. But what motivated the nostalgia, and what compelled them to participate in the reunion so eagerly? What did they accomplish by meeting their classmates at the reunion? In the accounts John and Betty related to me after the reunion, we find different answers to these questions.

Gauging Progress

John is the music buff who selected the phrase from the Don McLean song for the reunion motto. He thought the image of the "rolling stone" best describes his own life after college, as he has fumbled to latch onto a job on which to build an adult career. At the time of the reunion, he was working in a printing company in town, but he considered it temporary, a way to make a living while he searched for a better opportunity. He told me that he had recently become discouraged and wondered if his plans for his future were realistic.

Several weeks after the reunion, I visited John in his one-bedroom apartment at the edge of the town, just a few blocks from the mall where the reunion was held. After inviting me in, he apologized for the paperwork spread about the living room. He had resumed his neglected job search, and his apartment had become a "battlefield," as he put it, for writing job applications and fine-tuning his résumé. Resuming the job search, he explained, "might have something to do with the reunion. . . . I don't know, but . . . I feel sort of invigorated after that. It brought back the mind-set to try again."

■

John's Story

The reunion was a funny experience in many ways. It kind of takes you back to a time in your life that you'll look back on as you get older. The problems which made you suffer when you were in school look a lot simpler now, compared to the ones you have now. The problems you had then might have seemed to you as big as the ones you have today do now, but that is only because that was the world you lived in then. In fact, in ten or twenty years, the

problems you have now might not seem as bad as the ones you'll
have then.

But some bad memories from high school don't go away. I
noticed that there were many late apologies and late confessions
made at the reunion. "Well, it's kind of too bad that happened, but
we were kind of young then"—you know. I also noticed that people
were telling other people, "Boy, I had a terrible crush on you and I
just felt awful about not ever doing anything about it." I think as
you get older you get a little less inhibited, and, besides, you don't
have to see these people again, you know. You don't have to live
with it. So you feel that you want to say it, just to get it off your
mind, and whatever the reaction is, you don't really care! I'm sure in
high school if you'd have done that to somebody and they'd have
given you a bad reaction, you'd have been mortified for six months!
You couldn't face anybody! I think when you're that young, you
make a lot of mistakes and you don't know how to confront people.
In a way, college makes you grow up a little bit in that regard,
because you go to college and you realize that you're just one out of
thousands, and it's up to you to get it done. Nobody's gonna be
there to make sure that you get through. Nobody guarantees that
you will be okay.

I don't know about other people, but I sometimes dream about
my high school days. The dreams are mostly ones in which you're
sitting in class with people, and you're sitting exactly where you
were sitting in class. It's amazing! You're just sitting there, griping
like you used to do, you know: "I don't want to do this!" Basically, I
was more concerned about studying until I got into the university,
and then I just sort of took a break after that. If you wanted to get
into that school, you had to maintain a fairly decent grade average.
It was really a big deal to me, because I was going to be the first one
in my family to go.

My father was an electrician, and my mother didn't work. I
didn't know how difficult it was to be going to college. I felt, for
some reason, that it was just all going to be ridiculously hard. So I
was always a serious student when I was in high school. Not a real
partier. I kept a low social profile until my senior year. But in my
senior year in high school, when you've had your tests, your ACT

score, and all that business done, and you know that you're going to the school of your choice, then you kind of lighten up a little bit and kind of enjoy your last year a little bit.

So my senior year was the most enjoyable year for me, because I had everything set up, and I was reasonably sure that I was going to the university I wanted to. By the middle of the year I found out that I definitely was accepted. So at that point I started to become involved in class activities. I was on the student newspaper staff. We didn't have a big staff, so we had to work hard. We had one period of class every day for that, plus we had a lot of outside work. We had to go get the ads, and we had to get the copy ready, and all sorts of stuff. One guy from our class and I, we took care of a lot of photography for the sports. It was pretty time-consuming, but it was interesting. Ever since getting out of college I've been employed one way or another doing writing. But it was when I worked on the newspaper staff that I really got started at learning how to do it, and I just continued to do it. Even when you absolutely feel that that's the last thing in the world you want to do, you have to do it. The student newspaper was where I first experienced that.

There's another thing I remember well. We had a thing at our high school called "Class Night," and it always happened right before you'd graduate. It's where you do a series of skits and parodies on the people in your class, or teachers. I was in a couple of skits and worked on different phases of the production, coordinating many people so that the show moved along quickly. It was pretty fun. I got to know a lot of people that I really didn't have anything to do with until we did that. That was kind of a fitting climax for getting out.

I guess that my self-image kind of changed after that. I was not well known before then, basically because I didn't hang around with the real popular people. You know, when I was in high school it was very fashionable to come from this particular end of town, basically in the area around Washington Avenue on the south, and between Vanness and over to Oak Street. That was sort of the "in" community. People would strive, if they didn't live in some of those areas, to be with some of those people. They were fairly affluent kids, most of whose parents were professional people, or in business. I didn't grow up with them. And, since I was studying most of the time, I was invisible to them. So my senior year, when I opened up a little, I changed from more of a pretty serious student to a more outgoing person.

It was kind of strange to see those people who I only see in my dreams, and to sit and talk with them in the reunion. You don't realize how long ago that was until you start planning something like this, and when it actually comes about, you sort of realize you're getting older; you've been out of school for ten years. Other people said the same thing. Especially after you've been out of college, time just seems to fly, and it really does!

Interestingly, the people at the reunion seemed to remember me only as an outgoing person, not a serious student. It figures, though, because they didn't know me when I was a serious student. Also, in the reunion, people would go back to specific things you did in high school, and they'd say, "Oh, I always knew you'd be doing something like that!" I received enough comments like that. People usually related what I am doing at the printing company and what I was doing when I was on the student paper staff.

But to me, my job at the printing company is a temporary one. After I got out of college I worked at a couple of different jobs. I was looking for a very specific type of job, a marketing and promotion type of job. I couldn't get it so easily, so I held several part-time jobs after college while waiting. I've been with this printing company for four years, and I still haven't found the kind of job I'm looking for.

In fact, about two years ago at this time, I was going to Miami, Florida, and I expected to be leaving here within two weeks. But when I got down there, they had some problems. The end of the story was, a company they had purchased was in terrible financial condition; in fact it was practically bankrupt. So it wasn't just that they couldn't afford to open another branch and hire new people, it almost brought down the whole firm! In a sense, it was nicer that I knew it before I actually moved down there. I would have hated to have moved down there and been out of work in two months! Especially in a city that you don't know. You just don't know how you're going to fare. But if a certain job situation had worked out, I would have been living a very different lifestyle by now.

Ten years ago, I didn't think that I would still be living here ten years later. I didn't expect to be doing what I'm doing now. Sometimes, I really don't know what I expected, or if what I expected was realistic at all. I expected to be living in a city. And I still expect to live there, because the type of jobs I am looking for are primarily in major metropolitan areas or suburban areas. I also thought I would be married at this point. I got serious with people a couple of times and then things didn't progress to the point where similar goals were shared, and it looked like there wouldn't be any point in getting married. One of those deals.

Talking to other people at the reunion, the economy looks pretty bad everywhere. I always thought our class in general would do pretty well, because there were a lot of university professors' kids and the school as a whole was geared toward college education. But a lot of people, even those who were considered to be the most successful, have not succeeded to the point where I thought they would and are not real satisfied with the way things are going in their lives. So, in a way, I was a little more satisfied with the fact, knowing that other people are in the same boat.

But on the other hand, you also saw people at the reunion I just couldn't believe! They just happened to be at the right place at the right time and managed to get the jobs that they were looking for. I wonder sometimes how they got it! It seemed that people got serious about settling down and going to work, especially after they got out of college. Of course, there were some people who you wondered if they'd ever settle down. We joked a lot about our student activists. Bill Roberts used to be the consummate hippie of the class, and he just has turned around totally. If you had known Bill back then, you wouldn't believe how he looks now. Bill in a shirt and tie! That does not make sense at all! Bill now works for an insurance firm in Chicago, and everybody joked about it, too. But I thought to myself, hey, let's face it: you can't get along in the world if you don't conform, at least to some extent. And the more you conform, probably, the better you might live. Of course, I knew someone who looks out of the ordinary is not going to be accepted in general unless they've got something just outstanding to offer. You just can't. But in the reunion, I noticed that the people who are making it are the ones who turned totally around. There were some people who acted and looked like the same high school kids, but they haven't gotten anywhere. You can't go around looking totally different or acting weird and be a success. We couldn't live like that forever.

It was funny, really, that it happened in our class that some of the most outlandish people turned out to be some of the most serious ones. And some of those people . . . I kind of wondered, though, whether or not to take them seriously, because what they believed in then and what they seem to believe in now are totally different. I thought, well, was this person real then, or are they real now, or are they just playing another game? But, overall, we're all progressing, and most of the people would be settled eventually, and I'm just in the middle of the pack.

I heard everyone on the committee say that when this one is over, we'll never do it again; we'll let somebody else do it. Cathy and Janis got all the stuff and the money from this reunion, so technically they are in charge of our next reunion. But Cathy just lost her job, and I don't know what will happen. I imagine that in four or five years we may be ready to have a reunion again. It was kind of fun. But I'll never know what I'll be doing at that time. Because right now, as I told you, I'm beginning to get involved in a job search again, and I expect my lifestyle to change rather shortly. It kind of waxes and wanes. I expect myself to be married and to live in a big city at that point, but I can't be sure about it because of the way the economy is and the way lifestyles are changing. I do think, though, that things will change as soon as the economy turns around.

If I can somehow manage to get out of this town by that time, I would assume that I would come back to our fifteenth reunion, provided that the money situation is all right and that I'm not burdened down with house payments and things like that. I know some people from the class who felt that that was a real good reason not to come to this reunion. They felt too strapped by the payments and they just couldn't afford to spend the airfare. In my case, I will probably have my family living here for a few more years, so that would be another enticement to come home, too. I would probably arrange a vacation around that time. Because, you know, whatever memories you may have about high school, or whatever you may be doing five or ten years later, it's very good to see those people again. Even if we are doing totally different things now, we had some common experience in school together.

If we are to understand John's story, we have to read between the lines. His seemingly innocuous statements are often belied and contradicted by a tense, sometimes even harsh and sarcastic tone that runs throughout his narrative. What we see in his reunion experience is the manipulation of meaning for a specific biographical purpose: to come to terms with—and overcome—the fact that he has not achieved the adult success he had envisioned for himself in high school.

In John's account, we find a man who in high school chose and dutifully followed a standard American script for success, and now feels betrayed by that script. In high school, John drove himself, studying hard in order to enter the local university and thereby rise above his working-class background. Having no idea how difficult college would be—no member of his family had ever attended college—he prepared for the worst, studying to the point of having no time to participate meaningfully in high school social life. His desire to attain a middle-class lifestyle also separated him from his "flower children" peers, who defied the very ideals he hoped to achieve. For his hard work, John was rewarded with a bachelor's degree from the local university. In his mind, he had followed the script earnestly and had done all the things that are supposed to bring middle-class success. And yet, ten years after high school graduation, not only had the future he envisioned in high school failed to materialize, from his point of view he had not even begun to move in that direction. He was still stuck in Champaign-Urbana, without a career or family of his own. Struggling through a succession of unsuccessful job searches, John's current situation was one of uncertainty.

The primary biographical project John brought to the reunion was to see how life really works: that is, to see concrete examples of how his own peers are getting by, and to possibly find the key to success that had so far eluded him. It is significant that in his descriptions of the classmates he met at the reunion, John tends to categorize his peers as either successful or unsuccessful. And his notion of success is settling into a stable well-paying career, which in turn should lead to having a family and home.

This biographical project may be an important one, not only for John, but for members of his generation in general. Although it has now become conventional wisdom that the baby-boom generation will be the first in American history unable to enjoy greater prosperity than their parents, in 1982, when the tenth-year reunion of the Class of '72 was held, this trend has not yet been noticed. John, like many of his peers, tended to attribute his difficulties to the recession that was under way at the time, but the events of the past ten years have demonstrated that this trend runs deeper than any one recession. This issue of success is complicated by the fact that in the 1960's and early 1970's many of John's fellow baby-boomers had called into question the meaningfulness of American middle-class ideology. Furthermore, at the time of the reunion the Class of '72 was still in what Sheehy calls the "trying twenties," a period that is generally considered to be a difficult one in the American lifecourse.

What is striking in John's account is the way he describes the relative degree of success he observed in his classmates at the reunion, and the factors to which he attributes their success or lack of it. In his account, John identifies essentially four types of people. Of those who succeeded, there are those who "just happened to be at the right place at the right time" and there are "hippies" who had "turned around totally," succeeding by submitting to conformity. Those who are not successful are either "normal" people, like himself, who he sees as being held back by the poor economy, or hippies who still look and act the same as they did in high school. Yet his interpretation of the status of his classmates is but one of many interpretive possibilities. Shifting perspective slightly, one might respect the hippies who John says "haven't gotten anywhere" for standing firmly by their counterculture values in the face of a popular swing to the right. Similarly, those hippies who turned out to be successful might be seen as having simply applied their youthful passion and the skills they acquired as activists to adult careers. They may see no contradiction between their high school selves and their current selves. As for the "normal" people who succeeded, one might attribute their success to hard work and talent, rather than to luck, and those "normal" classmates who have not succeeded may simply lack drive or talent; perhaps they are the same "bland" people they were in high school.

John's assessment of his classmates is grounded in his own complex ideological dilemma. Coming from a working-class background, he was raised to believe in the American cultural script of the work ethic— work hard and you shall be rewarded—and the value of higher education in attaining a middle-class lifestyle. The stagnation he feels he is experiencing calls into question the validity of the path he has taken. Contradictory statements contained in his interpretation of the lives of his classmates reflect this ideological confusion, as well as his struggle to derive from the reunion the meaning that is best suited to himself.

In John's account, while he sees those hippies who stayed the same as losers who never grew up, he nonetheless seems to consider those hippies who succeeded by becoming "normal" to be hypocrites for abandoning their idealism. "Was this person real then," he asked, "or are they real now, or are they just playing another game?" For John, the former hippies are symbolic figures whose post–high school life confirms the rightness of the ideological choice he made in high school. And yet he seems to contradict himself in the next breath, when, in speaking of those "normal" people like himself, he attributes the success of some not to hard work and perseverance, but rather to luck.

In pinpointing the cause of his own perceived stagnation, John again seems to contradict himself. His final word is that the economy is to blame, and yet he seems unable to shake the nagging fear that the real cause lies in his own inadequacy, as he resumes his job search with even more zeal—almost desperation. Again, he seems to doubt the work ethic even as he is unable to free himself from its persuasive power.

Perhaps John had been harboring this doubt since long before joining the reunion committee. Even as he worries that he should be working harder, he is tempted to give up the struggle—if only temporarily—and try to recapture the pleasure of those last few months of high school by joining the reunion committee. But the experience of attending the reunion gave concrete shape to his fears as he faced his peers from high school. He seemed to find it somewhat bitterly ironic that his classmates did not remember him as a "serious student"—the image of himself that he has striven to cultivate in adult life—because such students are, almost by definition, socially invisible to their peers.

Rather than understanding John's current struggle in terms of his high school aspirations for a better life, John's classmates, to his disappointment, referred back to his most visible high school role—a member of the student newspaper—and saw his current job at the printing company as a natural outgrowth of his high school talents. His peers' assessment of his current status—"Oh, I always knew you'd be doing something like that!"—not only renders his earnest study in high school meaningless, it feeds his fear that this might really be the best he can do.

John demonstrates a complex mix of cynicism, fueled by self-doubt, and optimism. Through talking with his peers at the reunion, he discovered, to his relief, that the poor economy was holding many people back, and that there was nothing particularly "wrong" with him. This may explain why the success of some of his peers in spite of the bad economy seemed to him to be largely a matter of luck; there was nothing particularly "right" with them. As soon as the economy turns around, he predicts, both he and his friends will find success. John goes so far as to predict that he will be married and living in a big city by the time the fifteenth-year reunion rolls around, despite the fact that he currently has no concrete prospects in either love or work. He speaks almost with a sense of envy of those who could not attend the reunion because "they felt too strapped by [house] payments." He imagines that he, too, might not make it to the next reunion if he is "burdened down with house payments and things like that." Otherwise, he adds, "I would probably arrange a vacation around that time." In a sense, he has made those who could not attend the reunion his own role model for the near future.

Staging a Character

Like John, Betty attended the local university and never left Champaign-Urbana. In contrast to John, however, she feels her life is more or less "established." She met a man in her senior year in college and married immediately after graduation. She is a nutritionist working at the university's cafeteria, and her husband is a city bus driver. The couple plans to start a family in due course, but at this point, "we need to save some more money before we are ready for kids."

I visited Betty one evening in her modest two-bedroom house located in a newly developed housing project on the outskirts of town. Immediately after we exchange greetings, before I have a chance to ask my questions, Betty excitedly launches into an anecdote.

◼

Betty's Story

I have something interesting to tell you. I met a girl at Weight Watchers who was in my high school class. I didn't realize before the reunion that she was going there. She's one of those who live in town but did not come to the reunion. So I started telling her about it and told her who all were there, and she was so mad that she didn't go. She received the invitation, but she said "Nobody would know me. I wasn't anybody in school, so why should I go to it? People wouldn't recognize me." I told her she was crazy. I never thought I knew so many people until I went there. At the reunion, you knew everybody. I talked to everybody. I told her the names of some of the people who were there that I knew she knew. She said she could not believe that those people were there. Now she's mad and disgusted. She asked me to bring the pictures I took at that reunion so that she can see what they look like. She said next time, no doubt she will go. She was nobody in particular—she didn't run around with those who ran around, you know, popular girls who hung around with guys. She probably didn't stand out, but there were a lot of us who didn't go out with guys or anything like that in high school.

I didn't have any idea what would happen. I kind of expected that we would be roaming around talking to people. I never expected, though, that it would be like that Bell Telephone commercial for calling long distance. In the commercial, one guy is telling another on the phone about all the people from the class whom he saw at the class reunion and saying, "Hey, you're missing those people." I didn't expect it to be like that, but it was. I expected that people would be really different from what they were. But most of them acted the way you'd figure they would. The ones that were louder then were always loud, and the ones that were quiet, sitting back in school, were quiet and sitting back at the reunion. I might have been a little louder at the reunion than I was in high school, but this was because I knew what we were doing. I was involved in the whole event as a committee member, so that I could talk freely to everyone if they asked questions. So I probably talked more than I normally do. I would have been the quiet, shy type, like the girl whom I met at Weight Watchers, if I hadn't been involved in planning the reunion.

The reason I got involved in the reunion committee was that I really wanted to see those kids. When I graduated from high school, I guess I didn't realize, hey, this is it! You aren't gonna be with these people whom you've been with for a good number of years, some whom you've been with twelve years, all the way from elementary school. All the life you remember, you've been around them. And all of a sudden, hey, it's gone. You'll never be with them again! At first it was really a shock to me, because I really didn't realize that it was going to be like that. Going off to college, you do forget high school because you've got another group of friends to go around with. But, once in a while, you start thinking back and saying, gee, I can't wait to see them at a reunion to see what everybody is doing and what's going on in their lives. I'm sure some of them wanted to come back just to brag about what they are doing. But in my case I just wanted to see what some of them are like. I kind of missed them.

So when John called and told me about that radio announcement, we decided, okay, now's the time. Since at least January a year before, whenever we got together, we kind of fancied seeing those kids at a reunion. Actually, just between John and I, we thought things out about what we would like if we ever got hold of people in the class. But we simply couldn't figure out how to get a group of people together. When John contacted Mary, she said that there had already been one meeting and mentioned ten names of people who were there. John called me back and said, "They're going to have another meeting soon. We'd better get our stuff ready and go in there and tell them what to do." He also said that "judging from the way she sounded, they don't know what the hell they're doing." By that time, I had all the food figured out, I had collected prices from five or six restaurants in town, and I knew which place we would suggest.

So we got our stuff and went to the next meeting. There were only four or five out of the ten people who were at the first meeting. The rest of them just didn't show up! In the first meeting, they divided up index cards with the names of classmates among them, which I thought was pretty smart. But some of them didn't come to the second meeting, and there was one guy in particular who never came back to the other meetings. So in the first month or so we had trouble getting organized because we had to go and get the cards from those idiots! But the committee itself did flow. We generally had Mary, David, John, and me who you could count on being at the meeting. Other than that, you never knew whether Cathy or Janis would make it. There was a lot of work to do, and we all worked hard. But getting the basic things done . . . John and I feel like we were the ones who really did organize it.

What I was the most concerned was to get everybody back. I said that I wanted us to write in an invitation letter that we were inviting *everybody*. If we had received a letter from our class to return to Mary Walker, we would have wondered if everyone was invited. Mary was in a certain clique with a bunch of other kids. Seeing her name might scare some off, believe me. She was the type who ran around with jocks and cheerleaders. Actually, I don't think she had been with any of the guys from the team, but I gather that most of the people had heard of her. So both of us, John and I, said that if people saw our names on the committee they would get the idea that everybody was invited. Now we may say, "Oh, Mary isn't all that bad," but ten years ago she really acted like a snob. Maybe she's a different person now, or else we see her in a different light.

The committee itself was composed of a lot of oddballs. None of us were actually close in school except John and me. I would say that Mary and David were pretty close, and Janis and Cathy might have been. In fact, it was the best thing about the committee: we were mostly from separate groups doing separate things in high school, so we all knew different types of people. That's probably the reason why we were able to get so many people's addresses.

You know, in high school we had different types—football players, jocks, and intellectual types. And there were guys who rode motorcycles and had cars who were considered not so smart. They ended up dropping out of high school and getting jobs doing auto mechanics or working at gas stations. And there were your weird ones, the ones who were almost always at the park nearby smoking dope. We had all different types of people at the reunion. This surprised me, because I always thought that it would be the football players and cheerleaders who would go to a reunion. But there were also a few greasers, like the guy who showed up in the army uniform. I never expected someone like him to show up. And there were some of the weird ones. Most of them seemed to have gotten pretty normal. Most faces which I remembered as pretty wild looked terribly conservative now. They looked like they had done a 180° turn. Do you remember the girl who was voted the "Most Eligible"? She was strange. I think she was one of the types who hung around with greasers. Nobody remembered her at all. Everybody went home and looked her up in the yearbook, but she didn't even have her picture in our senior yearbook. Everybody, especially guys, were asking, "Who is she? Who is she?" Mark Williams, our class clown, is another one who has changed a lot. He's gotten very conservative. He showed up in a shirt and tie. It just doesn't fit his image. He just got a promotion in a law firm in which he's working. I saw it in the paper.

There were some shy types, too. There was one of my girlfriends who was even shyer than I was. She never went out and always stayed home. She wasn't in anything. I was in the band; that saved me. Being in the band, I was at least out. We had concerts and ball games, so we did get out and have fun. But she was very, very shy. I think she probably came to the reunion only because one of her best friends wanted to come and dragged her there. I know she left quite early. Yet I imagine that she was glad she finally did go. I can see why some people, like her or the other girl whom I met at Weight Watchers, wouldn't want to come to the reunion. They didn't think that they were anything in class, and maybe they did want to see the other people and to hear about what some of the others were doing, but felt they aren't doing anything for themselves now. It's hard to tell, but maybe they thought that they haven't made names for themselves yet to show our classmates.

My high school memories are filled with a bunch of

disappointments. I don't remember anything thrilling. I had fun playing in the band. My favorite things were marching band and going to all the football games. Unfortunately, my class was the only class in recent times which could never beat Oak High School in football. What a disappointment! I remember that in our senior year the game was played at Oak High, and when we were coming back to our school after the last game, which we hadn't won, some of those guys, the big football players, were crying their eyes out. They were crying because they hadn't beaten Oak all three years that they were in high school. That's something you're *supposed* to do. You can't understand this unless you went to Elm High. We still get sentimental about our old high school when the Elm fights with the Oak. If you've been raised in this town, it's always there. My dad graduated from the Oak and he brought me up loving the Oak. So, when I was little, I always wanted to go to Oak High. But once I got into Elm, it was, "Sorry Dad!" Even now I support Elm High. I have yet to go to an Elm-Oak football game since I've been married, because my husband is from the Oak and he wants to sit on the Oak side and I don't!

A lot of disappointment with guys—that's another thing. I could never get to go to a prom or something of that sort. I feel like I've missed something by not getting to go. Back then, and probably still now, guys are the ones that are supposed to ask you, and if you're not asked . . . I never went out on a date. Compared with the rest of the girls on the reunion committee, I'm probably the only one that didn't get to go to a prom or on a date. Unbelievable! I rationalize this by talking to John. John is like a big brother to me, and I think I'm probably like a sister to him. We can talk about stuff like that. I have discussed this with him many times. I always ask, "How come our girls never got to go out? What was wrong with us?" He says, "I bet it really wasn't anything wrong with you. It's just that you girls all stayed together in a group, so guys didn't come around you." John at one time confessed to the fact that he had almost asked me out for our senior prom. I had always dreamed of going to a prom, but we girls ended up doing other things because we waited but didn't get invited. Once we broke up and went our separate ways after graduation, something happened.

I think we got a little better. My best friend, Kate, who was even quieter and shyer than I was, was the first one of us to get married.

So at the reunion, I personally made sure that I went up to the guys that I used to like, even though they may not like me. There were four guys in particular whom I wanted to see, and one of them didn't show up. They all probably fared the way I figured they would. They all looked pretty decent to me. Well, no: they looked a lot older. I didn't expect them to be like that. Ralph, he used to have long, long, blond hair. The color of his hair has changed, and he's lost a lot of hair, too. He's now the father of a three-month-old. There was another guy, Steve. He was probably the one I was closest to. It was in junior high when he was playing in the band with me. So I really knew him. We could talk to each other just like yesterday at the reunion. But he's the one who dumped me for a succession of girls. It was just one after another, and I always wondered why he dumped me. So I asked him about it at the reunion. He doesn't remember exactly why, but we could talk about all sorts of things, and I now know he liked me. He's married and has a five-week-old baby. I was curious to see his wife, but she was not there because she had to take care of the baby. He's doing all right, I guess.

One of the other two guys I think I scared off—oh, no, I didn't scare him off; it was one of my girlfriends who did it. It was too bad she didn't come to the reunion. She was in the band with me, and I had confided to her that I liked this guy. Then she went over to him and told him. What a big-mouth! You see, I had five or six classes with him within one year, and he was sitting next to me, and we talked a lot. But all of a sudden, he found out that I liked him and, Jesus, he shied away. "Help!" You know. But when I walked up to him at the reunion, he asked me what I was doing, and I asked him what he was doing. He said that he had gotten married last August. "Oh, August when?" I asked, because I had gotten married in August, too, although that was four years ago. He has turned out about the way I figured he would. He is handsome. He hasn't changed so much.

I met my husband when I was a senior in college. My husband is a city bus driver. I went to the university in town and I lived at home all four years in college. This meant I didn't meet any guys at school. I was in home economics, and there weren't any guys in those classes. I didn't meet many people, period! I worked at the concession stand at the movie theater over on campus all four years at college, every Friday and Saturday night. That's probably why my social life went downhill. I didn't have anybody to go out with on the weekends, except that I went out with those people who worked at the movie theater after work. Anyway, I rode the bus all the time to school and then to work at the movie theater over on campus, and he was a bus driver. And lots of times he drove in the evenings and lots of times I would ride it back to campus to go to work at six o'clock at night, and there was nobody riding the bus. I was the only person on the bus. So I talked to him. One day, I forced myself and asked him out, because we got free tickets to go to the movie by working at the theater. I just asked him if he wanted to go to a movie. We went to a movie and we kept going out. We first went out in January—my last semester in college, thank heavens, because otherwise I never would have made it through college. I was paying more attention to him and not enough to what I was doing in school.

Kate's husband was thrilled about seeing all those guys who Kate always talked about. My husband could have cared less about seeing anybody. I had to drag him to go. In fact, Kate and her husband came over here before the reunion and told him they'd kill him if he didn't go. Finally, he decided that he'd better go, because he didn't want to fight. He didn't want to go because he didn't know anybody except Kate and her husband. But I didn't want to go alone, either, because it seemed to me too much trouble to tell everyone that I'm married. Easiest thing to do is to just introduce my husband, or even just his physical presence would be enough to let everybody know that I'm married, you know. My husband is older than me. He graduated in '63. His twentieth-year reunion will be next year. I don't know if he's going to go, though.

Nobody at the reunion actually told me that I've changed, but I know I have. I became a little more outward in college for some reason, but I don't know why. And then, if you talk to my friends I work with now, they wouldn't believe that I was quiet and shy. And after talking to those guys whom I used to like, I think that they probably liked me, but they just didn't say or show it. Ten years ago, I never would have thought of talking to them that casually. I was surprised at the ways I interacted with the people in general at the reunion, too. I couldn't imagine myself acting like that toward them ten years ago. They might have thought that I've changed, too, but they just didn't say that to me. No matter what they thought of me, I felt that I became a different person that day.

Betty's story is more straightforward than John's. She is more frank about her motivation for joining the reunion committee, and about her feelings about reencountering old friends. Moreover, the subject matter she chooses to include in her story differs drastically from that of John's, and the difference is striking when we consider that John and Betty have been close friends since high school. While John sorted out politically active "hippies" and "normal" people as a basis for current status comparisons, Betty never even mentions the word "hippie," and makes only brief reference to the "weird ones" who smoked dope in the park. Although she is intrigued by the "180° turn" she perceives some of them to have made, the comparison of career advancement does not concern her much. What figures prominently in Betty's account is a preoccupation with the internal social structure of high school peer groups and her struggle to overcome her former identity as a shy, high school "nobody." Her story is almost ahistorical, in the sense that it presents a classic description of the American high school pecking order. Categories such as jocks and cheerleaders, motorheads and greasers, as well as such episodes as losing the "Big Game" and not being asked to the prom, transcend the particularities of her generation as well as the social circumstances in which she finds herself today.

At the core of the Betty's story is her identification with the image of the "nobody." Beginning with the story of the high school friend she met at Weight Watchers, Betty repeatedly associates herself with classmates whom she characterizes as high school nobodies, such as her best friend, Kate, who was "even quieter and shyer" than herself, those shy classmates who did not attend the reunion, and her friend who left the reunion early because she felt uncomfortable. Betty also defines her nobody image by contrasting herself with Mary Walker, the chair of the reunion committee, who in high school was socially active and, from Betty's perspective, snobbish.[1] Betty finally identifies with the unspecified nobody she imagined might be scared off at seeing Mary's name on the reunion invitation. By putting her own name on the invitation, Betty felt she could demonstrate to others who had felt excluded from the in-crowd in high school that they were welcome, too.

Throughout her narrative, we see the image of the "nobody self" emphasized and amplified, given an almost mythological importance in accounting for her high school experience. For Betty this image is a symbol—a personal myth, if you will—used to underscore the internal growth she feels she has undergone since high school as she gained self-confidence, became sociable, and settled comfortably into young adulthood.

The fundamental high school experience that seems to have shaped her notion of herself as a nobody was never having dated boys. Today she feels she has outgrown that high school self, and has demonstrated to herself—by initiating her relationship with the man who is now her husband—that she has overcome her shyness toward men. But Betty needed to have that feeling of having changed confirmed and validated by "those kids" who knew her then. The reunion offered an opportunity to do just that: to stand face-to-face with the high school classmates who were the major force in shaping her adolescent self-image and show them the "somebody" she has become. By staging a new and improved character,[2] and actively eliciting reactions that would validate her current identity, Betty hoped to bury the nobody image that remained in the memories of her high school friends, and thereby convince herself once and for all of the authenticity of her growth.

For Betty, her tenth-year class reunion was a testing ground for her personal growth. But rather than simply show up and be tested passively, she actively joined in creating the setting and defining for herself what the content of the text will be. Becoming a member of the reunion committee provided her a strategic advantage that would alleviate any trepidation she may have felt about facing the challenge. By acquiring in-crowd status at the reunion, she was able to rise above the other "nobody" classmates and create for herself a comfortable environment in which to achieve her biographical goal.

In her own evaluation, Betty was even more successful in staging her character than she had expected. The mere "physical presence," as she put it, of her husband at the reunion bolstered Betty's performance by serving as a powerful demonstration to her former classmates that, regardless of how they might remember her, she was in fact capable of "getting a man." But the most dramatic moment in her reunion experience was talking with the men she had been attracted to in high school. She was not terribly concerned with obtaining explanations of why they had "dumped" her or not paid her any attention; the very action of walking up to them and exchanging innocuous chitchat as if they were old friends was evidence enough of the self-confidence and maturity she had gained over the last ten years. By staging her recently acquired self-image through her interactions with high school classmates, she actually became what she staged, and confirmed and validated her new identity. "No matter what they thought of me," said Betty, "I felt that I became a different person that day." The episode she described in which she met a fellow "nobody" at Weight Watchers powerfully confirms this new self.

In thinking about high school reunions, Americans often seem intrigued by the question of who attends and why. There are two popular assumptions. One asserts that it is those who enjoyed high school—and are unsatisfied with the present—who go to their reunions in order to relive their "glory days." The other common view is that it is present status—and the desire to show that status off—that motivates people to attend.

Reflecting this cultural concern, two psychologists (Lamb and Reeder 1986) carried out a mail survey, which they claim corroborates the first view. In comparing the characteristics of those who attended and those who did not, they found, contrary to their expectation, that the two groups were almost identical in terms of age, sex, marital status, and level of education, but those who attended their reunions consistently rated themselves as having been happier and more popular in high school than did those who did not attend. Using educational level as the barometer of social success, they submitted that "it is apparently not true that the main reason people go to reunions is to show off how successful they have become."

If we are to apply this dualism of past and present status in accounting for reunion attendance, John and Betty both seem to belong to that category of people who are least likely to attend their reunions. Betty's high school memories are "filled with a bunch of disappointments," while John's present life is not one he can show off to others. Nevertheless, both John and Betty are reunion enthusiasts who not only attended their reunion but actively worked to create the opportunity to meet their high school classmates. In fact, during the course of my research I met many Americans like John and Betty, whose biographies and motives for attending or not attending their reunions did not fall neatly into either the reliving-past-glories or the flaunting-present-success category.

How can we resolve this discrepancy between the dominant discourse and concrete experience? One serious flaw in the popular cultural viewpoint is that it neglects the power of subjectivity in shaping the individual experience of the reunion. In the context of the reunion, individuals assess their present life only in relation to their high school past. Betty, for example, is happy and comfortable with what she has achieved today, but seen from the perspective of popular American definitions of success, her marriage to a bus driver nine years her senior and her job at a university cafeteria would probably not be considered grounds for showing off to classmates. In the context of Betty's biographical development, however, her present circumstances—or, more specifically, her present *character*—take on a greater meaning. Furthermore, as I hope to demonstrate in Chapter 5, the meaning of the past can be redefined throughout one's life. In order to understand the motives and experiences of one person who attends or forgoes a particular reunion, we must understand the way in which the reunion intersects with the individual's biography.

John's and Betty's stories provided concrete cases for examining how individuals create meaning from their reunion experiences—meaning that serves their own biographical ends. We learned from John and Betty that reunion participants are not simply passive recipients of messages encoded in ritual performance, but rather are active agents who bring to the reunion some kind of biographical project—implicit or explicit, unconscious or deliberate, large or small—and act to shape and manipulate their reunion experience. High school reunions, by virtue of being ritual performances, work to produce a collective consciousness, and yet the effect is not uniform from individual to individual.

Those Who Have Shared Us: Reunions Across Time

> For one thing is certain as we grow older: The few people who have
> truly passed through us and us through them, until the dreams,
> images, memories are past sorting out, these people become
> precious links to our continuity. . . . If we try to bury the images of
> others who meant so much, part of us dies with them. How much
> greater our aliveness if we can come to a freestanding friendship
> with those who have shared us.
>
> —*Gail Sheehy,* Passages

In this chapter, I present the story of the fortieth-year reunion of a
World War II–generation cohort, the Elm High School Class of '42.
The experiential texture of the ritual performance and the affective
climate of this reunion differ in several notable ways from those of the
tenth-year reunion of the Class of '72 (Chapters 3 and 4). Such differences are derived from the significance people attribute to their high
school past and the role that past plays in the ritual performance. The
ritual performance of the Class of '42 brings the past to the fore, and
reaffirms and celebrates the existence of a community to which they
belong and can periodically return home to no matter what kind of
adults they have become. I will give special attention to how the telling
of the past as performed in the ritual evokes memories and reflection,
and causes a sense of the "Good Ol' Days" to emerge in postceremonial
conversation among the participants.

Catching Up

The Class of '42 is a group of "Depression babies" and one of the oldest high school cohorts whose adolescent years were affected by World

War II. The attack on Pearl Harbor took place in December of their senior year. "The war changed us from being sort of carefree to kind of serious," recalls Bob White, a member of the reunion committee and the Master of Ceremonies. "And the last six months of our senior year was very threatening. We knew we were going to go sometime and we're watching somebody go. . . . We didn't know when or what was going to happen to us." Patriotism embraced the whole school. Some members of the class entered the service without waiting to graduate, and many joined the military immediately after graduation. Those who enlisted during their senior year were given diplomas when they returned from the war. The war took four young lives from the Class of '42, and obscured visions of the future for those who returned safely after two to four years of military service. Jim Crouse, another committee member, said: "In our junior year, people were talking about the war going on in Europe, and I toyed with the idea of joining the military as soon as I graduated. I never gave too much thought to the future because I just assumed that it was going to have to be postponed, and I never started thinking about university until I got out of the service." The war meant big changes in the lives of young women, too; for the first time in American history, they were attending college in greater numbers than men, even counting those men who went to college on the G.I. Bill.

Despite the shadow that the war cast across school life, the school routine continued as always. Sports were as popular as ever, as was the school play, assemblies, the prom, and the homecoming dance. The "Sadie Hawkins Dance" was "always a big thrill," as one class member put it, because it stood the mores of the time on their head: instead of the boys asking the girls to be their dates, it was the girls who asked the boys. Dating, mostly double or group dating, was an important aspect of social life in school. Some class members ended up marrying classmates (five couples), while some others (seven) found mates in the classes ahead of or behind them.

"Back then when I was in high school, it was an altogether different moral climate," said Mr. White:

> I'll show you how mores have changed. It was when we were freshmen in high school, there was a big scandal. "Andy is smoking ciga-

rettes!" It was just a real alarming thing. We couldn't believe such a thing could happen! But today, even twelve-year-old kids in high school, 90 percent of them probably smoke more than cigarettes. I can remember one girl in school that got pregnant. But it was only one out of all the girls we had in school. But today, I don't know how many girls—I'm ashamed to ask them.

One aspect of student life at Elm High that has not changed much is the existence of a pecking order and cliques among the student body. One of the most comprehensive distinctions drawn is that between the children of university professors and the other students.[1] "It was sort of a caste system, really. Those university kids, kids of university people, they thought that they were better than the rest of us, and, you know, we were just coming out of the Depression, and their dads were making more money than those of us not connected with the university," said Jim Crouse:

> Don't get me wrong. They would speak to you, some of them would, but socially they had their own group and the rest of us had ours. There were some bad feelings among different groups of people. Sometimes people knowingly selected each other. You think, "Well, I've got to associate with this person because he's just like me, but this guy here, his family is a lot richer than mine, so I can't associate with him." You know, some of the kids felt superior to others. I think this prevailed more then than it does today.

Because of the lingering effects of the Depression, many students worked after school. Mr. White, for example, caddied at the country club, sold newspapers, worked in highway construction, and did yard-work. Many who had to work said that while they didn't resent the work itself, they did resent the fact that work prevented them from participating in after-school social activities, because participation in extracurricular activities was the main avenue by which students could achieve broad recognition and popularity, and many of the exclusive cliques were formed through clubs. "You have to be active in order to be accepted," said Mr. White. "I wasn't envious of other kids who didn't have to work, but it kept me from what I wanted to do. I was disappointed because I always had great expectations of playing football. I would have been a great football star. Oh, well, I don't know if I would have been. But I've always felt bad because I didn't get the opportunity, because I had to go off to work for my 33-cents-an-hour job."

And yet, he added, "a lot of other things dictated your action, too." Charisma and physical attractiveness enabled some to cut across class boundaries, while a lack of such assets made social outcasts of others. "I was a sort of class-clown or comedian type," said Mr. White. "I was always cutting up and making people laugh. I was taking things very casually and wasn't serious about anything. I came from a very poor family but it didn't bother me. I associated with the wealthiest kids in the class and the poorest kids in the class. I just didn't care." Mr. White remembered one shy, overweight girl who always stood apart from the other students, and he wondered if she would come back to the reunion.[2]

This is only the second reunion the Class of '42 has had in the forty years since graduation. Their first was twenty years ago. In fact, they decided at the twentieth-year reunion that they were going to have a twenty-fifth-year reunion, but no one took the initiative to organize one. Mrs. Smith, treasurer of the reunion committee, explained:

> Fifteen years ago, we were still busy with our families. But this time, it's been twenty years since the last reunion. We see others having class reunions and we are getting older and we've got to do something before it's too late. So several of us who see each other from time to time started to talk about having a reunion several years ago. But we said, "Let's wait a few more years, because 1982 will be our fortieth anniversary." So we got together one day last August and elected a president, treasurer, and secretaries and got the ball rolling.

The committee comprised seven men and seven women. Apart from the fact that all live within twenty-five miles of Champaign-Urbana, they do not have much in common in their present lives. Despite their proximity, they seldom see one another in their everyday lives. "We might run into them once in a while, like at the supermarket, or our children's school," Mrs. Smith told me. "You see, some of our children go to school together." The deaths over the past few years of several classmates who lived in the area heightened the survivors' sense of mortality. Mrs. Smith: "We've all gone to the funeral home. And each time we've all said we shouldn't let this happen. We should see each other more. But then we are all too busy with our own everyday lives and we just don't. Nobody makes the first effort and we just drift away again. It takes something like this [organizing a reunion] to pull us back together again."

The biographical situations of committee members are diverse. Bob White, an insurance agent who considers himself and is considered by others to be a smooth talker, was elected to be the president of the reunion committee and Master of Ceremonies. Alan Jones, a university administrator, opened his home for committee meetings. Jim Crouse, a self-employed businessman, was enlisted by Mr. White to be "class detective," and successfully located many missing classmates. Of the three men who are now retired, one is a retired fire chief who is active in the local Lions Club and another has a second job and is simultaneously organizing a reunion for his Army outfit. Two of the women are married to Elm High alumni: Joyce is a housewife and Elizabeth is now retired after working for the telephone company for thirty-eight years, and she and her husband spend their summers in a vacation home they bought in Minnesota. Mabel Brady is married to a rural mail carrier and has been working as an administrator in a nursing home for the last eleven years. Brenda Smith is a housewife married to an electrician and is active in her church. Hal married Evelyn Gebhart, a classmate, a year after graduation. Hal owns a furniture upholstering and refinishing business and Dorothy is a supervisor in the telephone company. Both served on the committee. Most of the secretarial work, such as typing and mailing letters, as well as preparing name tags and decorations, was done by the women.

The committee had a total of six meetings. "But we didn't do any work," Mrs. Smith told me. "We got it all assigned and somehow it got done in between meetings. We all wanted to catch each other up on what had been happening. So we just talked and talked about our present health and our kids. We reminisced a lot but we didn't dwell on it." The members of the committee all emphasized how much they treasure the friendships they renewed through organizing the reunion. For those who served on the committee, "the reunion will be more of an anticlimax," said Mrs. Smith.

There were 156 men and women in the Class of '42. By the time of their twentieth-year reunion, 14 had died, including the four men who died in the war. For their fortieth-year reunion, the committee began searching for former classmates using information in the booklet they had printed for the previous reunion, but locating classmates was much harder this time than it had been twenty years earlier. For one thing, there were fewer relatives or acquaintances still in town who could provide current addresses of classmates who could not easily be found. When the committee put an advertisement in the local newspaper in October, 45 classmates were still missing from the reunion address list. The ad brought in some new information. Since many classmates had attended the local university, the search was extended to the university's alumni club. Further, Jim Crouse, who frequently makes out-of-town business trips, located some of the missing classmates through phone books he found in hotel rooms. Finally the committee located all but ten classmates. Of the 138 people the committee had located, seven had passed away since the previous reunion. In fact, one of the men who served on the committee died of a heart attack several weeks before the fortieth reunion. In the information he had provided for the reunion booklet, he had listed one of his hobbies as "Antiques—collecting them, not becoming one."

Updating information for a new reunion booklet was one of the major projects undertaken by the committee. "We took this very seriously," says Mrs. Smith, "because even if some people cannot come, they are all asking for information about their classmates, where they live and what they are doing now." The committee sent out a questionnaire with the reunion announcement asking questions about children, education, military service, work, past and present residence, homes, travel, honors, memberships in organizations, and hobbies.[3] Ninety-six classmates responded to the questionnaire.

About sixty classmates have made reservations for the reunion. Including spouses, as well as six former teachers and their spouses, a total of some one hundred people are expected to attend the reunion. And there will be many coming this year who did not come to the twentieth-year reunion. "We have more time and money, I guess," said Mrs. Smith. About half of the sixty classmates expected to attend now live outside their home state. Some are planning to fly in from California or Florida. One man is expected to come all the way from Thailand, where he has worked for the past eight years as manager of an overseas branch of a major American electronic company. In fact, he was so enthusiastic about the prospect of seeing old friends he sent a five-hundred-dollar donation to help with the reunion expenses.

"This time, most of the people who are coming back are making a special effort," said Mrs. Smith. "Because twenty years ago, they had their parents or relatives who live in town and whom they wanted to see anyway, but now when they come back there's no one else to see but high school friends. It costs them more because a lot of them have to fly in and stay at hotels." Another major difference between the twentieth-year reunion and the fortieth is that more classmates are attending the reunion alone because they have lost a spouse over the last twenty years.

In organizing the event, the committee decided to do some things differently than they had at the twentieth-year reunion. For the reunion site, the committee searched for a place that had a special meaning for them in high school. The twentieth-year reunion had been held in the historic hotel in town where the Class of '42 held its senior prom. But twenty more years have turned the hotel into a shabby place, and they did not want to let it sully their fond memories. So for the fortieth-year reunion, they chose the country club that had been the center of much after-school social life, and the place some class members had worked as caddies. "It's kind of being nostalgic going back there," says Mrs. Smith.

Instead of the kind of small orchestra they had for their twentieth year, they will have a piano player play some tunes that were popular when they were in high school; they learned twenty years ago that the real fun of the reunion is talking to one another, not dancing. Besides, says Mrs. Smith, "dancing may be fun for twenty-five- and thirty-five-year-olds, but at our age it's a waste of money."

They also considered giving two or three prizes, fewer than at the twentieth-year reunion, but decided to simply give out a few door prizes. "We just didn't think that that's a sensible thing to do at our age," Mrs. Smith explained. Instead of award-giving, they have chosen to do some fun stand-up performances of the kind they did in high school, in an effort to bridge the gap of forty years. These will include readings of the class prophecy published in their senior yearbook and selected articles from the school newspaper. The class prophecy play-fully predicted what classmates might be doing forty years after gradua-tion.[4] "I was supposed to be a star radio entertainer. I was witty," said Mrs. Smith. For the newspaper excerpts, some committee members went to the high school and searched through huge piles of dusty, discolored papers lumped together in a storage room.

Another change is the size of the name tag. "We made it a lot larger than the one we had last time," Mrs. Smith explained, "because most of us need glasses to read fine letters."

The summer evening of the fortieth-year reunion of the Elm High School Class of '42 is bright and pleasant. Just as I park my car in the lot of the town's only country club, a BMW pulls in. In the car is a nicely dressed middle-aged couple. The woman, wearing a blue dress, checks her appearance in a mirror she has taken from her small handbag. The man, in a white jacket with a handkerchief peeping from the breast pocket, gets out of the car first. The man says, "Hi," and I respond in kind, but he seems curious about my presence. When he notices I am carrying a camera he asks, "Are you a newspaper reporter?" I explain briefly why I am there. "That's the most interesting subject I've ever heard of," the woman exaggerates. We walk toward the clubhouse, maintaining a comfortable distance from each other. The couple does not talk much, but I overhear the woman say, "Gee, I am nervous. Does it show?"

As we enter the clubhouse, we find a small space in front of a reception desk packed with early arrivers. Some enthusiastically ex-change hugs, kisses, and long-time-no-see greetings, while others look around for anybody they can recognize without the aid of a name tag. In line ahead of me, the woman I entered with brightens as she spots a woman in a flowery print dress working her way through the crowd calling, "Rose! Rose Stevenson!" Her husband looks on, smiling, while the two women hug and kiss, saying to each other, "I can't believe it. I can't believe it." "It's been a long time since anybody called me Steven-son," says the woman, as she turns to her husband. "Doug, this is Barbara, um . . ." "Parkins," says her friend. "I've been married for thirty years now. Come meet my husband."

This gateway to 1942 resounds with many such high-spirited rediscoveries of old friendships. Mr. White, a tall, handsome, gray-haired man with a fine physique, stands beside the reception table, extending a hearty welcome to all who enter. He is attired in the school colors: a red jacket and a black pair of pants he bought just for this occasion. "Jimmy Richardson, how are you doing? Hey, you're looking good!" Mr. White greets each classmate without a moment's hesitation, addressing each by the correct name without fail. Later, Mr. White will confide in me that the night before the reunion, he carefully studied the yearbook and the class picture taken twenty years ago: "I wanted to make sure that I would not embarrass them and myself by not recognizing them. To make them *all* feel welcome, I thought, would be the most important responsibility of the president of the reunion committee."

For many attendees, it is the first or second time since graduation they have seen one another. For them, the anxiety about whether or not they will recognize their classmates—or be recognized themselves—is even more intense. Mrs. Wilson, an attendee from Texas, will later tell me, "I was thinking to myself, 'How will they look?' 'How will I look to them?' It's a funny thing. Life is strange; you only remember your high school acquaintances as they were in high school when you don't see them in the period of forty years." Aging is an inescapable fact for the Class of '42; many participants will later comment that it was much harder to recognize people by appearance than they had anticipated. Mr. Clark, an engineer from Indiana who attended for the first time, will say: "As I was watching the people who came through the door, I was struck by how old everybody looked. While many of them looked very good, well preserved, still, suddenly, they were older people. There are many that I could not recognize without seeing the name tags."

Some will report to me embarrassing moments in which they failed to recognize classmates, especially those with whom they closely associated in high school. Mrs. Wilson:

> When one of the fellas came up to me, I was very embarrassed. I was embarrassed simply because I didn't recognize him and the reason I didn't recognize him was because he had changed so drastically. It was absolutely incredible. He used to be a good-looking guy with beautiful blond hair. He's absolutely bald now, not a stitch

of hair. I looked at him and he looked at me, and he said "Jonesie!" and I said, "Huh?" I was embarrassed, and he said, "Doug Warren." Of course I hugged him and kissed him, but I was doubly embarrassed because he realized my embarrassment!

If not being able to recognize others isn't bad enough, it is even worse to not be recognized oneself. In interviews after the reunion, many will relate to me the joy and sense of self-worth they felt when they were remembered. Jim Crouse will describe one such instance:

> I had an apprehension of how people were going to act toward you as much as anything else. But many people came to me and shook my hand. That makes you feel good, especially when somebody you weren't that close to remembers your name. Like that big tall guy—he could see anybody in the room, but he came to me and had his hand out, when he was three or four people away from me. That makes you feel good that somebody does remember you and will take time to come over and say "hello."

Remembering and being remembered: the two constitute the admission ticket for the reunion. It is through mutual remembrance that group membership is certified and participation in the reunion becomes meaningful.

The cocktail lounge begins to buzz with reuniters catching up. Everyone there, including me, wears a red name tag trimmed and printed in sharp black. Classmates are distinguished from guests by a cardinal— the school mascot—printed on the right-hand edge of their name tags.

A woman in a striped, one-piece dress shows family snapshots to a long lost classmate.

> "Our oldest is thirty-eight, Sandy. She lives in New Jersey, outside of Philadelphia. And my son Mark. The woman standing next to him is his wife. And they have two sons."
>
> "My children are all scattered, too. One is in Michigan, one is in Florida, and my youngest daughter is in Colorado. We have only one daughter. We're very proud of our children."
>
> "You know what is nice about having our kids in so many different places? We don't have to worry about where we want to go for our vacation."

As the two women continue to chat, their husbands drift away to look over an exhibit of class memorabilia that includes their senior yearbook and clippings from the local and high school newspapers. The headlines refer to various athletic and musical achievements of the Class of '42: "Big Twelve Football Champs of 1940," "E.H.S. Wins Five Firsts in District Music Contest." These headlines, together with the pictures of classmates that accompany them, tell of the passage of time and affirm the sense that their high school days have indeed passed into history.

A little after seven o'clock, Mr. White asks classmates to gather for a class picture. "Only classmates!" While class members are out on the green, a silence prevails in the clubhouse, where spouses sit awkwardly waiting.

After the picture is taken, dinner is served. The tables are decorated nostalgically. On each table is a green plant in a red plastic container with two pom-poms—one black, one red—standing in the soil. In front of each plate is a paper doll in caricature wearing a graduation cap. On the plate itself is a red-and-black reunion program on which the lyrics of the Elm High fight song are printed. There is no formal seating arrangement. Attendees may sit wherever they wish, but as classmates seek out familiar faces, the social groupings of their high school days reassert themselves after forty years. Jim Crouse will later comment, "If you had known us in high school, you would have noticed that at every table were close friends. That Betty, the girl from California, the one that was so bubbly—you see, she was the drum majorette. And that blond, she was one of the baton twirlers. They were very close, so they sat together. The athletes sat together, and then a few just sat because we had no place else to sit."

Each table comes alive with excited conversation. At one table, class-mates are passing around the class picture taken at the last reunion, twenty years before. They are trying to see if they can identify faces in the picture, commenting on who is here and who is not. Their conversation flows as follows:

WOMAN 1:   Where in the heck is Ned? He was here at the twentieth reunion. [pointing at the picture]

MAN 1:   I don't know. Somebody said they thought maybe they were moving.

WOMAN 1:	From where to where?
MAN 1:	From near Milwaukee to some place in Arizona.
WOMAN 1:	Last I knew he was in California, wasn't he?
MAN 1:	No, I don't think he was ever in California. He was in Kansas City for a long time.
WOMAN 2:	Is that the one we used to call Shorty? No, that's his brother, isn't it?
WOMAN 3:	Oh, yeah, I remember Ned. I didn't until you mentioned it though.
MAN 2:	Did someone talk with Lois Madson recently?
WOMAN 1:	I didn't talk with her, but I heard she's divorced now and is going to marry a guy two years younger than she is.
WOMAN 3:	Really? She was married to a college professor, wasn't she? I met her husband several years ago at a restaurant in Chicago. They looked happy then. What happened?
WOMAN 1:	I don't know. I heard that they were having problems for a long time and . . .

After the exchange of information on the whereabouts of absent classmates, the conversation shifts to discussions of how people have changed or not changed and the concerns of aging they all share today.

WOMAN 1:	I'm trying to place the guy sitting at the end of the table next to us.
MAN 1:	Yeah, I can't either. He looks familiar, but I can't place him. Isn't it strange how profiles do a better job than a full face? When we got out of our car in the parking lot, there came this man and lady. I introduced myself and he introduced himself and I couldn't believe that it was Pete Norman. He's aged quite a bit!
MAN 3:	I think the youngest-looking one in the whole bunch is Jack Simpson.

WOMAN 4:   He does. He looks beautiful. He's got all the original characteristics, too.

MAN 1:   I didn't think about it until I saw our graduation program hung up there on the board. The presentation of the senior memorial was done by David Welch. He's been doing memorials every day since then, you know: he's a funeral director in town. Did you notice?

WOMAN 1:   Oh, he inherited his father's business?

MAN 1:   Yeah, I heard that he is doing very well.

WOMAN 3:   May I see that picture? [pointing at the class picture from the twentieth-year reunion] Oh, I need glasses.

MAN 2:   I didn't wear glasses until I was forty-five, and then I started wearing them and I've been wearing them ever since. I just don't take them off anymore. I used to wear corrective lenses for close work and reading. And I spent all day doing this [stretches his arms back and forth] until one day I was in a meeting over with the Park Service in the park and I took my glasses off and this half fell to the floor. It broke right in the middle. And that's when I got bifocals.

WOMAN 2:   Have you had the experience of your eyes recorrecting? Mine are back almost to where they were when I first got reading glasses. I got these nine months ago and already the only thing I can do is to read a little bit out of the bottom. If I—

WIFE 2:   So you have bifocals?

WOMAN 2:   Yes, but my eyes have corrected themselves somewhat, so at a distance I see better without them.

MAN 1:   I think that's a good story. I'd stick with it.

Aging looms large in the catching-up discourse. "Who would have thought," Woman 1 will comment later, "that we would be talking about bifocals with these folks in high school? This alone gave me a sense of how different we are now, and it's *really* been forty years."

Performing Memories

On the stage, Mr. White steps up to the microphone. "Now, I don't want to talk too long," he begins, and a classmate snaps back, "Good!" The Class of '42, who remember Bob White as never being at a loss for words, bursts into laughter. After welcoming everyone on behalf of the reunion committee, Mr. White comments on the importance of high school friendships.

> I know that we made friends in each town in which we have lived, each neighborhood in which we've lived, and each job that we had. All those circumstances created new friendships, which played a very important part in our lives. But of all the friends that we have made, I don't think any had quite the same meaning or can take the place of the friends that we made in high school. And as I look out and see all of you tonight, I can see that certainly things haven't changed. In watching you and looking at you, I think that there is something almost magical about high school friendships. [A class member claps his agreement.] I know that whenever I speak with one of you, you're forever eighteen years old and running up and down the halls of Elm High School. And I think that's the pleasure of having remembered old friends. [Another classmate claps.]
>
> You know, I heard someone say once that a class reunion was when a lot of people got together to find out who was falling apart. [The audience laughs.] And I think that may be true of many classes, but it certainly isn't true of our class, because I think you all look just great. I checked you all over when you came through the door [laughter], especially the girls. I didn't see anybody that seems to me like they were falling apart. And I know that at present I would know everybody that came in tonight. I made a bet with some of the committee members. I said that I would know everyone that came through the door tonight, every class member that came through the door. And I would have won the bet—I lost—but of all the people Jim Crouse came walking in wearing a necktie, and I just— [The audience howls with laughter.] If it hadn't been for him, I would have won.
>
> I had a rather vivid illustration about—oh, I guess it was a cou-

ple months ago—that assured me one of our class members hasn't aged an inch in, what, forty years now. Johnny Thompson and I stopped in the Embassy. Embassy's a little candy store. [The class members, knowing full well that the Embassy is a local bar, laugh.] We stopped in for a beer and we placed our orders and the bartender took our order and he turned around and came back and he made Johnny show his ID card. [laughter] Isn't that right, Johnny?

Mr. White introduces the piano player, joking that he was the only member of the twelve-piece band who showed up, and then he introduces me, "a young lady named Kay who's a graduate student at the University of Illinois, doing a thesis on high school reunions." He adds, "I don't know how anybody can do a thesis on this [laughter], but she paid her own way here this evening and I'm certainly happy she's here and I know that we'll all make her feel most welcome."

Mr. White then introduces the six former teachers who have been invited to attend the reunion as special guests: Miss Young, whose last homeroom graduated in '42; Miss Dayton, the very popular history teacher; Miss Nestor (now Mrs. Keller), who talks about her efforts to restore a plaque engraved with the names of "all you boys" from Champaign-Urbana who served in World War II; Mr. James, who "had a smile that made you think that he was really a . . . that he was a real good friend" (but whose class Mr. White never took, despite the fact that "I took everything Elm High School had to offer but girls' P.E., and I was trying to take that but Miss Young wouldn't let me"); and finally Mr. Miller, the Dean of Boys, who always made you feel "you'd been treated right," even "just after he gave you nine years of detention." Mr. White concludes his introduction of their former teachers by commenting:

> I don't know how many class reunions these teachers are asked to attend. I'm sure that probably each year at least one class has had their reunion and they're expected to go there and pretend that particular class is their all-time favorite of all the classes that ever went to Elm High School. And they have to pretend that each one of us is their all-time favorite student. But at least tonight it'll be easy for them because they don't have to pretend [laughter and applause].

One attendee, Mrs. Owens, will comment later that the class members were touched that the teachers came:

> They all looked older. I was already taken aback by how old our classmates look. And the teachers looked ancient, comparatively! They were really authority figures in those days. One hears now from our children that there is an enormous discipline problem that you have in schools, even in a town like this. We weren't like that at all. And it's funny to think that *we* are much older than *they* were when we were in school! And much more interesting than that is that they acted as if they are still our teachers, us their students! They were paternalistic, even after forty years. They say that they were very pleased that some of their students had succeeded and had good jobs and so forth.

On stage, Mr. White takes a moment to tell about the genesis of the reunion. He describes, with his usual humor and anecdotes, the many instances in which the idea of reunion was mentioned without result:

> Each time I'd see a class member and we'd talk, the same thing would happen. They'd say, "Hey, I got a great idea. Let's have another reunion." And I'd say, "Okay, let's do it." And six months later I'd see another classmate and they'd say, "Hey, I got a great idea. Let's have a class reunion." "Okay." Nothing ever happened. So one day I'm in my office and Johnny comes in and we get talking and pretty soon guess what he says? He says, "Hey, I got a great idea. Let's have another class reunion." So I said, "Okay," but nothing happened. But about three weeks later Johnny calls me on the phone and he says, "Hey, let's get together." He says, "If we are going to have one, we got to get this thing going. We want to work on the committee. It's been forty years and it's time we had another reunion." Well, I thought, "Johnny's been out in the sun too long or something," but I said, "Okay. We'll do it." But we still didn't do anything. So another month went by and Johnny called again, so now I realized that he must be serious. So I said, "Okay, let me make some phone calls and I'll get back to you."
> You see the mistake Johnny was making—he thought I knew how to plan a class reunion [laughter]. And, jeez, I don't ever want

to admit anything that I don't do very well, but he thought that I knew what I was doing, so I made some phone calls. I did know one thing that was quite important. I knew two things. I knew that you had to have a lot of good people to help you or you weren't going any place, and I also knew that you had to have a lot of girls on the committee [laughter]. So we got a few people together, and a few more came in, and pretty soon we had just a great bunch of people that were working together and forming this committee.

Mr. White then thanks each committee member by name, commenting briefly on his or her particular contribution, both tangible and intangible. Then he reads from some of the letters the committee received from class members they had contacted. The first, from Lily Phillips, implores the committee to "Please, please find Bill McVay [laughter]. I want to give him a big hug." "Well," responds Mr. White, "we found him, Lily, but he's not here tonight. But I thought, 'Hot dang, I'd be glad to take his place!'" "Anytime!" shouts Lily.

Mr. White reminisces about the *Cardinal*, Elm High School's yearbook, and his involvement in its production. He asks Evelyn Gebhart (now Singer) to read the "class prophecy" as it appeared in the *Cardinal* of 1942. Mrs. Singer takes the opportunity to first thank Bob White for his work on the reunion committee, and then to read a poem that also appeared in the *Cardinal*, and which was apparently written by a classmate:

Our high school days are over now.
Come seniors all, let's take a bow.
We've worked and played, had joys and fears
And sometimes shed a few hot tears.
With Cardinal, we all have learned
That everything worthwhile is earned.
Our hearts are young; we're not dismayed.
We face the future unafraid.

The class prophecy, too, is a poem, though far more contrived and far less serious. The original prophecy in the yearbook looked ahead *ten* years, to 1952, but Evelyn revises it to apply to the present. The following is an excerpt:

Knowing that our class is
One for all, and all for one—
Don't mind the puns;
They're all in fun!
In the year of nineteen forty-two,
We find the seniors at E.H.S.
Just barely skimming through
Those deplorable final tests!
Let's look ahead forty years,
And note the way our class appears.
In looks and manner, poise and style,
We're bound to change in this long while.
In the year of nineteen eighty-two,
Our school is faced with problems new.
Since airplanes take the place of cars,
Pedestrians take refuge behind bars!
To save space in crowded lockers;
And to get the new vitamin "XQZ"
We find Cary Hall, now a little stockier,
Preparing lunch capsules in a pharmacy.

                                        . . .

Amy Hauser is a much quoted commentator.
Peggy Stewart is now a reputed gossipator.
Society editor for *Chicago Sun* is Harry Gimbel. [crowd laughs]
The audacious Roy McNeil replaces Walter Winchell.
Cliff Roberts is fashion editor for *Esquire* magazine. [laughter]
Alan Jones has invented a car-washing machine. [laughter]
In Sterling Hayden's place, we see Arthur Wright.
Twin-city animal undertaker is Bob McKnight! [laughter]
Gracious—vivacious—curve-acious,
Is Annette Young, now a Petty Model.
Lily Phillips' gleaming white teeth
Advertise Squibb's toothpaste! [laughter]
(How'd that get in here? It doesn't rhyme!) [laughter]

                                        . . .

Among the portraits Ann Morgan has painted
Are many with whom we are acquainted.

"Woman with the Hoe"—Dolores Benson,
"Twentieth Century Juliet"—Kathleen Johnson,
"Harry, the Happy Hermit"—Harry Schneider, [laughter] and
"The Lone Wolf"—George Fisher. [laughter and applause]
As a result of her last romantic affair,
Dot Richards ends up playing solitaire!
Sally Owens and Elda Hart, in the movie arena,
Have far surpassed comedians Lorraine and Pauline.
Ginny Sullivan is leader of The Women's Symphony.
Marilyn Sadler, an opera star, sings the melody.
Evie Russo and Angela Kirsten now twirl
Their skirts as Ziegfeld chorus girls. [laughter]
Remember how Ann Rothman
Made Andy Hauzer pace the floor? [the crowd "ahs" in recognition]
Well, now a married man,
He is pacing even more! [laughter]
(Andy makes a lovely cradle tender, or rather tender cradler!)
[laughter]
. . .

Winner of the Kentucky Derby, defeated the men!
It's Evelyn Gebhart, a masterful equestrienne! [laughter]
Brenda Nemzhow is radio's star entertainer.
Jo Sacks is Barnum and Bailey's lion trainer!
Ring Master, George Rutledge, the performers presents.
Mary Ellen Kay, fat lady, is the first BIG event!
Roy Hampton is just one of the circus flunkies.
Flora Reynolds and Mary Russell perform with the monkeys.
Edna Barns, tight rope walker, creates a sensation!
Clowning is Larry Singleton's circus occupation.
Acrobat Maureen Willis floats through the breeze.
With Norm McVay, the man on the flying trapeze!
. . .

Louise Armstrong, a lovely star of stage and screen,
Has changed her name to "Cardinal Queen!"
You'd never know him, so we'll confide;
Pinky White is now a blond—PEROXIDE! [laughter]
. . .

Entertainers—Ray Walker and his men of rhythm.
Bonnie McKenny and Joyce Goldstein sing along with 'em.
[whistles from the audience]
One who deftly daubs the digits is Martha Jo Edgers.
One who should've gone west, is just a pest, Dennis Rutgers.
Murphy and Witts in a new V-8,
Crashed into a corn crib and met their fate! [laughter]
Clark McCloy and Bill McVay are still having fun,
Earning a living by the sweat of their tongues! [laughter]
                              . . .
Jim Powell, Charles Racer, and Chester Mussey,
Now occupy *cells* in the "Big-House" apartments. [laughter]
Judge Calvin Williamson, for murder condemned 'em.
Joseph Metz and Wayne Thomas as wardens attend 'em.
Earl Withers, it isn't hard to guess,
Has become a great political success.
Jimmy Crouse has grown to be six feet eight!! [laughter]
Margaret Pratt, Secretary of War, we congratulate!
Marv Lakey's fate we said we'd hush.
Mike Long's occupation makes me blush.
Harold Singer is a professional pick-pocket. [loud laughter]
"Doobie" Keats has invented a potent sky-rocket.
(The one that knocked the caps off the Japs.)
Edgar "Adolf" Kelly governs conquered Germany.
Tom "Benito" Meineke rules conquered Italy.
Dorothy Stanley is President over the Japanese domain.
And now that we are free, the world may live again.
Now that this prophecy is over and done,
We hope you, too, have had some fun.
Signing off for now—Your prophets wacky,
We remain, as ever—Kate and Kathy.

The putative future predicted forty years ago calls attention to the images of the individuals held by peers in high school. In addition to being reset forty years in the future, rather than ten, the class prophecy as read at the reunion differs in several other respects from the version actually printed in the yearbook. Most significantly, all references to deceased classmates have been removed, either by replacing the original name with that of a surviving classmate, or by removing the entire stanza or half-stanza in which it appeared. The names of four deceased class members are thus deleted. Another stanza referring to two class members who could not be located and were mentioned nowhere in the program is deleted. Another important change is the replacement of the name of a classmate who could not be located with that of Ray Walker. Mr. Walker did not actually graduate with the Class of '42, but he considers himself and is considered by others to be a member of the class. Mr. Walker was crushed when he was not invited to the twentieth-year reunion, so the committee members made certain to invite him this time, and have made him even more "official" by adding his name retroactively to the class prophecy. By revising the class prophecy based on the state of the class today, participants in the reunion are in effect reorganizing group membership on the basis of present relationships.

Forty years can give rise to groundless rumors. Before proceeding, Mr. White takes a moment to dispel one such rumor—a rumor that one of their classmates has died. Mr. White tells us that the classmate's mother called him last night and assured him that her son was still alive, though he could not attend the reunion.

Committee member Elizabeth Mead now takes the stage to read excerpts from copies of the *Horizon*, the student newspaper, published in 1942. The first piece comments on the resemblance between certain class members and comic strip characters such as "Maggie," "Jiggs," and "Tonto." Elizabeth gets bigger laughs with the second piece:

> [She quotes] "Hey, wouldn't it be fun to see Marvin Leighton without his new sweater?" [laughter] We had to wait forty years, didn't we? [laughter] "Harold Singer not bragging?" We're still waiting for that. [laughter] "Can you imagine Edith Penny five feet three inches tall? Don Nichols being quiet for five minutes? The Elm and the Oak on friendly terms? Miss Scott in a gloomy mood? Arnold Richetts with straight hair? Dick Shelton not sleeping in study hall? Mr. Webber not reading the *Courier* every day? Ray 'Frosty' Walker without his camera?" He hasn't lost his technique, though, we learned that a while ago, didn't we? "Jean Hendricks worried about

anything? [laughter and applause] Jimmy Crouse not chewing gum? Bob White without a word to say? [laughter] Jonny Robbins without a comic book? And Lou Bianchi without letters?" [applause]

Following a collection of "Did-you-know-that . . ." trivia on various classmates and teachers, and news items about sports and music awards received by classmates, Mrs. Mead reads the opinions of several classmates on the war in Europe as quoted in the *Horizon*:

> Now, as you all remember, World War II was on the horizon during our senior year. In the February 7, 1941, issue of the *Horizon*, several seniors were asked their opinion on the question, "Should we aid Great Britain in this war?"
> Jackie Webster replied, "I believe that the U.S. should strengthen her own defenses first. Aiding England might necessitate our entering the war, which might be otherwise avoided."
> Wilma Durst expressed the majority of opinions by saying, "I'm on the fence. I favor aiding England as much as possible as long as we do not hinder our own defense or become involved in the war."
> Brenda Nemzhow: "If England is to win, I think she needs our financial and material aid. I'm absolutely opposed to the idea of sending our men to fight for her." But the previous Christmas, Brenda wrote this poem:
>
> > "Will there be Christmas over there, with snow upon the ground?
> > Will it be quiet and peaceful, with only the merriest of sounds?
> > Or will there be airplanes bombing and killing civilians there,
> > And troops of soldiers marching into the night of nowhere?
> > Will there be Christmas here as we've always had before?
> > Thank God there will be, and, we hope, so many more."

Mrs. Mead concludes this segment by saying, "Now at this point in our lives, we didn't realize—for us and for the world—that we were heading into World War II, and that was the Big One."

"Then, on a lighter note," Mrs. Mead continues:
> The March 13, 1942, issue said, "Did you notice senior history

students looking rather pale Tuesday? Yon history quiz was the cause of the physical and mental disorder. Some of them looked even worse Wednesday when they received their graded papers back. And it must have been really a terrible test, because this is what Johnny Duncan wrote about it." The poem is entitled "Flunked." [laughter]

> "Once upon a midnight dreary,
> While I pondered, weak and weary,
> Very sad and very worried
> As through hist'ry notes I hurried,
> Vowing to ignore no more
> Those hist'ry notes until before
> The day the final's due.
> And so dawns morning, bright and fair,
> And I arise full well aware
> That I am not prepared to take
> A test 'bout dates and stuff.
> Quoth Mr. James, 'I cannot bluff.'
> There's no use lyin'
> Was lack of tryin'
> And I'm in the doghouse now." [laughter]

And some articles about fads and fashion were received with enthusiasm:

"A bow worn on the left side of the head means that a girl is definitely not interested in any boy in any way, shape, or form. A man-hater, in other words. A bow worn in the middle of the head signifies that the girl is going steady and there isn't a chance. But a bow worn on the right side means that a girl has no strings attached and newcomers will be welcomed. [laughter] Lily Phillips has a brand new coiffure, and part of it is a bow worn in the middle, but at the back of her head. Now here is the problem: could it be that the meaning is the same as when worn on the top of the head, or has Lily cooked up an entirely new meaning? We couldn't say, but it might be worth investigating."

Then the February 13, 1942, *Horizon* has this anonymous letter to the editor:

"What's this school coming to? First girls wearing knee-length socks. Then they start wearing slacks. Then the horn-rimmed glasses without the lenses followed by plaid shirts. And now they're wearing red sweaters and earrings. If Elm High had visitors, they might think that the girls around here were walking novelty shops. A group of senior girls started the red sweater/earring fad, but within a few days the fad will be picked up and will spread throughout the school. So as with all the fads started by the fair E.H.S., maybe more boys should get crew cuts, wear knickers and wool shirts, just to make the school looked cracked on both sides." [laughter]

[signed:] *A Senior Boy*

"Which one of you did it?" Mrs. Mead asked the audience. A member of the audience shouts "Ross Brown!" to which Ross Brown responds loudly, "No, I didn't!" This interaction produces a good deal of laughter. Mrs. Mead goes on to read an article about a mock trial, selected because it features the president of the reunion:

I'll just have to take time to read to you about Bob: "State of Illinois vs. Bob White. Charge: murder. Proved not guilty. Thirteen jurors voting on the thirteenth case of Friday the thirteenth failed to reach a verdict in civics class, but the vote was seven to six in favor of hanging Bob White, [laughter] accused of murdering his employer. Judge Dave Anderson presided over the slightly boisterous, but honorable, courtroom, and at times it seemed that the honorable judge would completely blow up and throw out both attorneys. State's attorney Homer Prather and his assistant Bill Hatter were much more conservative than defense attorneys Lester Sullivan and Ralph Comaroff. With the corny jokes pulled by the defense, it seemed that they were more interested in laughs than the acquittal of their client. Bianchi sat at Mr. Gibson's desk twirling the cylinder of a rather cute-looking 'hog leg' (and that's a gun, to you rookies). [laughter] White was very nonchalant on the opening day, just as nervous on the second day, and kind of mediocre at the last. His good looks may account for the six votes cast in his favor, since the jury was composed of eleven girls and two boys."

Mrs. Mead places the youthful incidents she has just read about in their historical context by reminding attendees of the prices of familiar things in 1942:

> Now, it was only 40 cents for the *Horizon* subscription, and you could start by putting 10 cents down. . . . Then the price of the prom tickets were as follows: the seniors were free, other E.H.S. students were 75 cents plus tax, and outsiders were a dollar plus tax. The *Cardinal* was two dollars before January 31st, but it went up to $2.25 January 31st. [laughter] Curlers were two dollars. Shampoo and wave, 50 cents. Then, to attend a movie at the Park, the Princess, or the Co-Ed, the matinee was 15 cents and the evening was 28 cents. [laughter]

Elizabeth reads a few more items before concluding: "Now, the *Horizon* was not the *National Enquirer* or the *Golden Star*, but we liked it at that time and we found precious memories in it now. So, to steal a phrase, I'll just end by saying, 'That's the way it was, and you were there.'"[5]

She returns the microphone to Mr. White, who reports the death, just three weeks before the reunion, of a committee member. After a moment of weighty silence, Mr. White announces a brunch to be held the following morning, made possible by an unexpected surplus of funds:

> We have about $475 left over, after everything's paid for. So we had several suggestions on what to do with it. One I thought made a lot of sense, and it would have been easy and wouldn't cause any problems—It was suggested that we just give that money to the Master of Ceremonies. [loud laughter] And we voted on that idea, and it was voted down. The vote was nine to one. [laughter] So we had some other suggestions, and someone suggested that we have a brunch tomorrow morning. So we voted on that idea. And the idea was approved. The vote was still nine to one [laughter], but it was approved, and that's what we're going to do tomorrow.

He explains the details and asks for a show of hands from those who think they will be able to attend. About eighty people—roughly three quarters—raise their hands.

The last formal event on the evening's program is a show of pictures. Rather than use slides, an opaque projector has been set up so that class members can show any photographs they happen to have brought along. Joyce Goldstein (now Fiske) gathers pictures from around the room and shows them with the projector. Explanations and comments are offered. This portion of the program generates a good many "oh"s and "hm"s, as well as sentimental laughter and applause.

When all the photographs have been shown, Mr. White announces that a number of door prizes will be presented afterward. "Johnny Duncan suggested we give away a book entitled *Sex After Sixty.* [laughter] Hal said there isn't such a thing. And I don't know whether he meant there isn't such a book, or . . . [laughter] But anyway, we didn't get such a book, but we are going to give away a couple of [prizes]."

Mr. White explains the organization and price of the class picture, and then, after promising to keep the reunion committee alive, calls Brenda Smith to the stage to read a poem she has written for this occasion. Her poem captures in capsule form the history of the Class of '42.

> I remember the Class of '42.
> My best friends are some of you.
> Was the time of the Cardinal, the scarlet and black,
> And I rekindle old memories as I look back.
> Now, our football season was long and tense.
> But we poured it on when we beat . . . *Ferrence!?* [laughter]
> With players like Bianchi, Elsworth, and Walker,
> When we got into trouble, we could always punt.
> But in basketball we were really great.
> By beating Oak High, we went to the state.
> We surely recall our famous foursome:
> Wurster, Douglas, Singer and Jameson.
> Then came Pearl Harbor, and our boys became men.
> Some, like Bob Green, enlisted right then.
> But most of us finished and graduated,
> But all of our goals were reevaluated.
> We went out into a world of turmoil and stress,
> All dedicated to do our best.
> For some, a time of adventure; our wings we were trying.

For others, it was just their time for dying.
Now forty years later, we gather once again.
All of us older, some not as thin.
But most of us closer, as we share and remember
Our high school days, as if only last September. [applause]

Reconstructing the "Good Ol' Days"

The postceremonial atmosphere is much more relaxed and cheerful, as class members begin to stray from their tables and visit each other. Some sing the Elm High fight song, accompanied by the piano. The tone of interaction has been transformed noticeably: the stiffness felt prior to the ceremony has melted away, and spontaneity, intimacy and nostalgia overtake the room. The content of conversation has shifted, too, from catching-up to remember-when. As one attendee will later put it, "They became almost as if they haven't been away from one another. They picked up right where they left off."

At one table, several classmates gather and recount memorable episodes from their high school days. It seems the ceremonial portion of the reunion has been effective, reviving high school memories and reconnecting participants to their shared past. Gradually, class members begin to reflect on the meaning of their high school days and mutually affirm the sense that those were the "Good Ol' Days."

ANDY: Remember the night you wrecked the old car?

TED: And you wrecked mine.

ANDY: And I wrecked yours.

Ted and Andy reminisce about a popular game they played in high school called "Ditch 'em." The game involved two cars, each loaded with a bunch of boys, and the lead car would try to "lose" the second car. In those days, Mr. White will tell me later, it was unusual for high school students to have cars, and it was not easy even to ask to borrow Dad's car. "It was a great adventure for us to drive around town without our parents."

TED: Al's dad had a '39 Chrysler. My dad had a Model A Ford, a 1931. My Model A Ford could come up to a corner and

make a U-turn, see, but this big car couldn't. So Andy
wanted to drive mine one night, so I drove his dad's. But I
hit some gravel, skidded, and broke a wheel. Well, the
next winter we were out and Andy was driving my car
then and he skidded on the snow and broke a wheel.
Andy had to tell his dad the first time that he was driving;
I had to tell my dad the second time that I was driving.
[Ted and Andy laugh]

MARY: You evened things up.

TED: Yeah, it balanced out. [He laughs]

ANDY: I'd forgotten about it. We had a lot of fun. God, we had
fun.

BOB: Remember the candy store where we used to hang out?
The place is a parking space now.

The candy store Mr. White is referring to holds a special place in
their memory, as he will describe to me later:

Back in those days, we had no money. A big, big thrill to us was to
hang around at a little confectionery, a candy store downtown. We
used to go in there after school or after I got through work or
whenever you found time. We went in there, and each of us bought
a Coke for a nickel and sat around the booth and made all these
plans. We always talked about building a great raft to go down the
Mississippi River. That was the dumbest thing in the world, because if we'd built a raft and gone sailing on the Mississippi River,
we'd have sunk. [He laughs] But that was something that we always
dreamed about in that candy store.

The conversation continues:

ANDY: So that place is no longer here, huh? [turning to Ted]
Were you there when we talked about going down the
Mississippi? [Ted nods] And who else was there? I
don't think Hal was, was he?

ROB: [Without responding to the question] I stole a record
from Hal's sister. A Benny Goodman record.

TED: Ah! [addressing Rob] You tell your sister we still have that Humpty Dumpty cookie jar we got as a wedding gift. We still have it in the kitchen. Thirty-three years. And we lift Humpty Dumpty by the head to get at the cookies.

ANDY: Kathy Roughton told me that she still had the wedding gift I gave her. Kathy is the oldest friend I have in the world. She lived across from me. She said to me today, "I cannot remember life without you." And I thought that was a nice way to say it, because if she says it like that, I'd say the same thing. I cannot remember life without Kathy.

DAVE: I think high school friends have really some special quality. Even if you might not see them no more than twice in forty years, and you might think that you aren't close to them if you didn't see them more often than that, but . . .

DICK: But it's easy. It's that easy. Pops right into place.

BEV: Like it was just yesterday.

HAL: Yeah, I'm so glad that I saw Dirk today. He probably doesn't know this, and probably this doesn't mean anything to him, but it means a lot to me. You know, Dirk comes from an affluent family. His father was a professor. And I come from a very poor family, but Dirk accepted me. And that was very important to me, to be accepted.

BARBARA: He's very nostalgic.

HAL: And well, I've become affluent. Not necessarily as much maybe as he has, but for me . . . At that time, I had nothing, absolutely nothing. My father left home in 1933, left a woman with three children who absolutely refused any support. She made it on her own.

BARBARA: I can relate to that. I raised three.

MARY: We were a pretty close class. I mean, you know there really weren't small cliques. We all liked each other.

BOB: Clark Gillman said it tonight, and I know he meant it: ours was a doing class. There was something going on all the time.

JOYCE: We all kind of worked together as a group.

MARY: I think we feel closer to our high school classmates than we do to any other acquaintances we've made, because they knew you when you weren't very much. I don't have to impress you, you don't have to impress me.

ANDY: One of the things about liking [our class], Bob. I always felt this way. We had such a hepped up college experience, most of us did. For those who went to college in normal times, it was just an extension of high school at a little more mature level, but we didn't have that experience. So high school played a very special part in my life. It is the "Golden Years" for me.

BOB: I went off to the Navy after school, and so my high school days were the happiest days of my life.

BEV: Some of us went to college together, but we were all in different fields and our classes were part and parcel. And those high school years are very important in the emotional makeup of people. We were maturing, we were going from children to adults.

MARY: It was a carefree time. Our kids may be better academically, but there's just so many things that distract from a happy young childhood.

BEV: Yeah, but *we* learned too.

BOB: Yeah, and, you know, I think there's an awful lot of success in our class. I had never thought about it until tonight.

BOB: Yeah, there are a lot of very successful people in our class.

ANDY: [calling to a woman who is leaving] You're not going away, are you?

WOMAN: Honey, it's past our bedtime.

ANDY: Now you're showing your age to me.

WOMAN: You bet . . .

BOB: I'm in bed by ten o'clock.

BEV: It's your bedtime, too.

BOB: I get up at 5:30.

ANDY: Do you think it's true that when you get a little older you don't need so much sleep? I don't believe it.

BEV: I don't believe it either.

MARY: I think you go through a period when that's true. It's when your bones are aching so much after you've been in bed six hours, you got to get out of bed and move. Haven't hit that period yet?

ANDY
AND BEV: No. I haven't hit that one yet.

MARY: Well, I bet if we took a little poll, I wouldn't be the only one who's in that shape.

BEV: I'm sure you're right.

By this time, many participants have left. Even after being asked by the management to leave, however, this group stayed on talking until past midnight.

Mellowing

The fortieth-year reunion of the Class of '42 and the tenth-year reunion of the Class of '72 differ in crucial ways that are related to both lifecourse and history. For both classes, a war is the defining element of their generational memory, and yet the wars they went through were very different. The Vietnam War had been with the Class of '72 since childhood, and was a political issue that divided the student body as it did the country as a whole. Growing up amidst the turmoil of national debate, youth, for this generation, was synonymous with resistance, protest, and defiance—a rejection of conformity and mainstream, middle-class values. In Chapter 3 we saw how this generational characteristic played out in the tenth-year reunion of the Class of '72: members were reluctant to acknowledge conformity, and as they struggled to succeed in their adult careers, they felt obliged to justify their current middle-class status or aspirations.

These experiences contrast sharply with those of the Class of '42. The attack on Pearl Harbor occurred just six months before graduation, abruptly interrupting the normal school life they had been enjoying. World War II, unlike the conflict in Vietnam, was a popular war, drawing the near-unanimous support of the Elm High Class of '42 and of the entire nation. But overnight the tone of high school experience changed drastically. Reflecting the positive national consensus, members of the Class of '42 whom I interviewed were by-and-large reluctant to voice any criticism of the war, but they nonetheless expressed resentment at having had the privileges of youth snatched away from them prematurely. Mr. White put it this way:

> The military brought me to places I'd never dreamed of ever being. I was associating with a bunch of guys who had never been away from home either. We were all doing things that we thought were great, but they were rather silly and immature. And when you came home you were not a kid anymore. I had aged quite a bit. I left when I was eighteen and came back twenty-two. Those intervening years were supposed to be a time you would spend doing whatever kids of that age do. Our age group didn't get to do those things.

Even some of those who attended college after the war dropped out because they had trouble readjusting to civilian life, and many who did complete their bachelor's degree saw their college education in strictly pragmatic terms. As one class member commented, their college experience was "hepped up"—not the period of youthful exploration that college is seen to be under ordinary circumstances. Because of their different historical experiences, the notion of youth generally held by the Class of '42 differs radically from that of the Class of '72. For the former, youth was that carefree time they enjoyed in high school until the war confronted them suddenly with adult responsibilities. It is this past that becomes the "Golden Years" that are retrospectively reconstituted in the reunion, through the performance of high school memories.

It is important to recognize, however, that historical events, such as wars, do not affect all members of a class cohort in the same way. Some find their "Golden Years" in another period of life. Such differences are created by the relationship of history to the individual's biographical development. Mrs. Grace Thompson, a school teacher and member of the Class of '42 who chose not to attend the reunion, told me her college years, not those spent in high school, were the best part of her past (she considers the present to be the best time of her life!). "I enjoyed high school tremendously," she told me, "but what happened in college superseded it." For Mrs. Thompson—and perhaps for many women of her generation—the war brought a sense of liberation, a loosening of traditional gender roles, as women were expected to contribute to the war effort by filling the vacancies left by men. College, according to Mrs. Thompson, freed her from parental and peer dictates about what is required of a proper young woman, and gave her an opportunity to broaden her horizons.[6]

Even among men who served in the military, evaluations of the past differ. For example, Mr. White and Mr. Crouse joined the Navy and Air Force, respectively, soon after graduation. But while Mr. White sees his high school years as his best, Mr. Crouse says that the Air Force is "where my heart really lies." Mr. Crouse describes himself as having been a loner in high school, but he found a profound camaraderie in the Air Force, where he shared virtually every minute of his daily routine, both on duty and off, with the other men in his outfit. After returning home, he entered college on the G.I. Bill, but difficulties in readjusting to civilian life led him to drop out. Since then he has never been able to establish a solid career, and has drifted from one job to the next. His experience in the Air Force provided him joy, a sense of self-worth, and powerful friendships; it was perhaps the only time in his life he felt truly a part of society. At the time I interviewed him, he was eagerly looking forward to a reunion of his Air Force outfit, to be held in Chicago two months after his class reunion.

Mr. White's account of his war experience is not so rosy. Most of the men in his outfit were killed in battle, and he keeps in touch with only one of the survivors; he finds the prospect of an outfit reunion laugh-

able. Mr. White was in the invasion of Normandy, and did a tour of
duty in the Philippines and Guam. "One night, we had half of the
whole crew's quarters knocked out by the torpedoes, and bodies were
just thrown over everywhere," he recounts. "I was there but I got out of
it. It was a war, so there were many, many terrible, terrible things. Of
course, there were some really good chances that I would have died. It's
kind of funny, but I never expected anything would happen to me. I
always expected to get home." He did have fun, admitted Mr. White,
but not the kind of fun he can now look back on with pleasure. In the
life story Mr. White related to me, the negative effects of the war on his
personality and future prospects are featured more prominently:

> I had a strange experience. As I said, I always enjoyed high school. I
> enjoyed making friends. I made a lot of friends in high school. I en-
> joyed making friends initially in the service, guys who were aboard
> ship. I can remember many of them. But so many of them got
> killed that I suddenly quit making friends. I became dubious about
> making friends. I didn't want to make good friends and have them
> get killed. I remember on my first ship I had a great bunch of guys.
> We were about the same age—eighteen, nineteen, twenty years old.
> I had a great time with them. But so many of them died. So when I
> was sent on my second ship, I didn't make friends anymore.

When Mr. White returned home from the Navy, he said, his personality had been changed temporarily. He had become very withdrawn:

> From the last year when I was in the service and the first several
> years I was back, I just kind of wanted to be left alone. I didn't want
> anybody to bother me. That was entirely different from what I had
> been. The things that happened in the service bothered me a lot af-
> ter I got home. I dreamed about them. The dreams were really bad!
> I don't remember how I got over it. I guess it's just time did it or
> something.

College had never been a part of Mr. White's aspirations even before
the war, and the Navy had not prepared him for a career ("Whatcha
gonna do in civilian life as a gunner?"). So after trying out several jobs
after the war, he finally found his niche in sales, since he had learned in
high school that his real strength was his "gift for gab." It is this ability

to speak easily and make people laugh, he says, that had enabled him to mix with the "popular crowd" in high school in spite of his working-class background, and it was his rediscovery of this talent after serving in the military, he says, that made him the successful salesman he is today. Mr. White told me proudly that in the previous year he had become the second agent in town ever to write $2,000,000 worth of insurance.

The effect of the reunion ceremony, however, was to minimize such differences in experience and to impart a feeling that high school had indeed been the "Golden Years" of every participant. Even Mr. Crouse, who had been ambivalent about attending the reunion, admitted: "I can honestly say that I enjoyed this one much more than the twentieth reunion. This one seemed like there was more old-time camaraderie or whatever you want to call it. People were a little gladder to see each other, regardless of who they were and what they are, than they were at the twentieth reunion."

Although differences in class members' experiences of high school and the war are certainly important, there is yet another element that embraces the Class of '42 as a whole: lifecourse position. For members of the Class of '72, adult life is really just beginning. They are still very much in a period of trying to pin down who they are and what they will become in adult society. Whereas "trying to be set" (Sheehy) may characterize Americans in their late twenties, the lives of the Class of '42 have long been set, and, their most productive years behind them, some are already retired. While there was a sense of insecurity and nervousness in the tenth-year reunion as classmates were reunited, attendees of the fortieth-year reunion seem to have had a much clearer understanding of who they are and what they have become, and they seemed more comfortable in dealing with old classmates. There was a certain amount of competition and status comparison, but for the most part members were supportive of one another regardless of who had become what. "We talked a lot about our children," commented one woman. "People were glad to know that somebody else's children were doing well, and so on. It was not so much a case of trying to compete through children."

Perhaps for those attending their tenth-year reunion, competition and comparison are an indispensable part of healthy self-development and the definition of career goals. Their future is perceived as vast, allowing plenty of room for correction, but for those attending their fortieth-year reunion, choices have narrowed or long since been made, and so they have a good sense of what they can and want to do to make their remaining years worthwhile. As Mr. White put it, "Twenty years ago, we were still trying to make it. We were all self-centered. Now, forty years later, we don't give a damn. Whether we made it or not, it's too late." They must come to terms, one way or another, with the consequences of commitments made earlier in life.

Thus, instead of status comparison and competition for the purpose of realigning pathways, there emerged in the fortieth-year reunion a sense of mutual affirmation and a consensus that they all had "made it" in their own ways. Reunion attendees emphasized that the class as a whole had turned out to be successful. Judging from the data given in their reunion booklet, the Class of '42 looks pretty much like a cross-section of the American population: attorneys, small-scale business-men, schoolteachers, housewives, salesmen, real estate and insurance agents, staff positions at the local university, a brakeman for the local railroad. A product of the Depression, the Class of '42—unlike the Class of '72—consciously and unashamedly strove to attain middle-class security, and accepts the results with grace.

Increasing age brings out a shift in the criteria by which personal growth is evaluated. In assessing individual biographical development, the focus at the tenth-year reunion was on the achievement of social status and changes undergone since high school, but in the fortieth-year reunion, biological aging and continuity are the primary concerns. Attendees of the latter reunion compare their own biological progression with that of others and earnestly exchange health-related information, but they have, for the most part, come to terms with their mortality. Some reported to me after the reunion that they had rethought the timing of retirement, while others expressed a new resolve to preserve or improve their health. Mr. Crouse, who has a history of heart problems, finally quit smoking after fending off the nagging recommendations of his doctor for years.

Aging is a blanket fact of life that covers the entire Class of '42, transforming "those high school kids" into middle-aged men and women. And yet, they claim, beneath the outward signs of age can be found those same kids they remember from high school. In identifying continuity in the complex of images of classmates, reunion attendees delineate the "original" characteristics that are still present in their aging classmates. Observing the physical changes of his classmates, one informant commented afterward, "The interesting thing is that there are certain aspects in which they changed very little. Personality was surprisingly constant. Another, it seems, is the way they do body language, and the other is their voice." This focus of attention on continuity often brings out an acceptance of others as unique individuals. Another informant described one such instance: "There were people who make kind of a big show, but that's just their way of doing things. Their natural way of putting on. There's one girl with white hair, I always thought that she was snooty. She talks a lot and makes a lot of guys an awful lot. But she is just that way. She always was. Nobody thinks anything of it anymore." In this way, characteristics that were once a source of conflict or competition are redefined and accepted.

In the case of the Class of '72, we observed that old animosities are still alive in the minds of participants and acted out as minidramas at reunions. The fortieth-year reunion provided an opportunity for class members to see that old high school tensions and conflicts—personal and structural—have melted away as members have matured. In speaking about meeting a high school rival, a retired university staff member commented:

> You know, this guy, I really hated him forty years ago, and now I'm glad to see him. I suppose in a way the past becomes the "golden days." Well, of course, the substance is not there anymore. For example, there's one guy I felt very bad about because I tried to get the leading part in the senior play, and I didn't get it and he got it. I thought he was too dumb to learn the lines. But he did it all right. But it didn't bother me anymore. We talked about the play, but he didn't remember it as well as I did.

Another man described meeting an old heartthrob:

> There was one [girl] that I was, God, I was terribly attracted to. But when I was in high school I was so shy and I was sort of afraid to really become serious or make advances. I used to fantasize a lot

about her and think of all kinds of excuses to talk to her. She did come to the reunion, and she is married to an engineer. But I found out that I had no feelings [for her] anymore. It was interesting, because by now we'd all grown up and one didn't feel shy; you could talk and express your feelings. But, of course, I didn't, because my wife was there and her husband was there.

Initially, the group divisions and class structure of high school reappeared in the way people seated themselves at the dinner tables. But this structure disintegrated in the nostalgic atmosphere of postceremonial conversation. Mr. Crouse told me the most memorable scenes from the reunion for him were those in which high school "nobodies" and "university kids" engaged in friendly conversation. "That tall guy and that white headed guy—[in high school] it was unthinkable to see them standing in the hallway chatting!" Having been a self-described "nobody" himself, Mr. Crouse was happy to tell me that no one failed to speak to him, and that he gained a genuine sense of equality— regardless of "what kind of money they are making now"—that he had not felt at the twentieth-year reunion. "It's no use trying to impress the people who knew you when you weren't very much anyway," he added.

In the tenth-year reunion of the Class of '72, the award-giving ceremony pushed to the fore the contours of the present lives of class members and provided the participants with a forum for collectively assessing changes and recent achievements. The ceremonial events of the fortieth-year reunion, by contrast, put the past on the stage through the telling of high school stories, creating an opportunity to collectively reassess high school experience. Instead of reviving old conflicts and animosities, the evocation of memories forced them aside and reconstituted a sense of the "Good Ol' Days" and of belonging to the community that shares that past. This shift in the meaning of the past may be understood in terms of the aging processes that members of the Class of '42 are all going through. "I'm sure you're still young, and old age probably does not enter your mind," Mr. White said to me, "I don't know what age it is, but there is a point to which you feel eternally young. But some point down the road you realize you're not a young person anymore. And you're not ever gonna be young again. So the things that you did when you were young take on a greater meaning."

Breaking away from the high school past is essential for younger Americans who are trying to become adults, but age eventually urges them to merge once again with the "root community" where their biographies originate.

This rediscovery of the root community seems doubly important for those who came back from out of town. For them, the passage of forty years has largely severed both physical and human connections to the area, as over the years their parents, relatives, and friends have moved away or died. Many expressed a sense of loss and loneliness. "I have no connection here," said a woman who came from Minnesota. "I wouldn't be here if it weren't for this reunion. There would be nothing here to bring me back to this town, and that's kind of sad but it's true." This is where "everything is in the past," said Andy, who came all the way from Thailand. "I had almost literally never been out of Champaign-Urbana until I went into the Navy. Grew up, born at home—actually born in my house on Pennsylvania Avenue—and all through school and freshman year in college." Most of those who came from out of town made a nostalgic tour of the area, visiting the old school building and taking photographs of their old homes. For these people, high school classmates, and the sense of community that emerges at the reunion, are the lifeline that maintains their fragile connection to their "old home."

The different quality of experience I find in the reunions of the Class of '72 and the Class of '42 is representative of a general time-patterning of reunion experience across the lifecourse. In fact, when we look at the Elm High School class reunions of different age groups—the tenth, fifteenth, twentieth, thirtieth, fortieth, and fiftieth years—we find a gradual change in the kind of ceremonial activities staged. In the earlier reunions (the tenth and fifteenth years), a concern with relative status and a sense of competitiveness is expressed, often blatantly, through award-giving ceremonies. On the other hand, as age increases, so does the enactment of the past—the high school past and the larger historical past—thereby promoting a sense of group identity and belonging. In the tenth-year reunion, elements from the past are suppressed in the construction of the event: The place they held their reunion—a shopping mall—was chosen for the sake of convenience and had nothing to do with their high school experience. The hall was decorated in the school colors, and images of the high school mascot were present, but beyond this no high school memorabilia were displayed. The music, too, was current, and not the rock 'n' roll of the late sixties and early seventies.

The twentieth-year reunion of the Class of '62 is typical of a transitional phase in which elements from the past begin to assume an important role. The past is expressed in high school memorabilia sold in an auction, in the showing of eight-millimeter films and slides taken during high school, and in the telling of high school anecdotes that are playfully interwoven throughout the ceremonial events.

The climax of the twentieth-year reunion was an auction staged in order to raise money for the next reunion. The items sold included their graduation program, a program from a football game that proved to be a major victory, old pictures from a talent show known as Class Night, as well as an old school pennant, a "Class of '62" mug, shoelaces decorated with the school mascot, and a T-shirt signed by every class member who attended the reunion. The auction started slowly but grew in intensity, taking on what was certainly an unplanned and perhaps not entirely unconscious meaning: by bidding on various class-specific memorabilia, which would have little or no value in any other context, class members publicly and often audaciously demonstrated their commitment to the class and to future gatherings. This was illustrated quite dramatically by the fierce bidding for the last item, the reunion T-shirt, which sold for an unbelievable $230.

In the thirtieth-year reunion of the Class of '52, the past firmly occupied center stage. A carefully crafted, chronological narrative of the senior year, entitled "The Way We Were," was read, in which major class activities were recalled month by month. Another, shorter account, entitled "Where We Are Today," was read by two women, one referring to memorable geographical locations of high school activities, the other telling what has since become of those same places. The contrasting images of Champaign-Urbana and its surroundings called attention to the passage of time. The concern with time was reiterated in the M.C.'s brief account of the significant historical events that had taken place in their lifetimes.

Only one award, "Farthest Traveled," was presented at the thirtieth-year reunion. In place of the elaborate award ceremony that is a feature of earlier reunions, a "Class Résumé"—a sort of demographic profile of the class, based on responses to a questionnaire—was read. Occupations, hobbies, places of residence were all quantified, but no one's name was mentioned. Though this ritual bears some resemblance to the award ceremony, in that it serves as a yardstick by which class members could measure their own position relative to the class as a whole, the anonymous approach provided a softer alternative to the award ceremony's often prickly tone and avoided singling out individuals for either ridicule or praise.

In the fiftieth-year reunion, we find a dramatic disappearance of all ritual activities. According to the president of the Class of '32, his class had held reunions every ten years since graduation, and in earlier ceremonies they had given awards, but this time, "none of the folks in the reunion committee felt like doing that kind of thing." Their formal program was limited to an introduction of guests (six of their high school teachers) and an acknowledgment of committee members. Beyond this, the closest thing to a ritual was the time set aside for class members to stand up, one by one, to state their name and the state they now reside in. Two members took this opportunity to ask the class at large questions of their own choosing: "How many people are coming to a reunion for the first time?" "How many of you still have living parents?" It seemed that attendees at the fiftieth-year reunion, for the most part, had risen above concerns of past and present and were content to celebrate together the simple fact that they all still had the vigor to attend a reunion.

I have outlined what I see as a general time-patterning that characterizes reunions throughout the lifecourse. We cannot neglect, however, the possibility that this pattern may simply be coincidental. Obviously the choice of reunion activities is to some extent an expression of the unique characteristics of a given class, of the personalities of those who gathered to organize the events, of generational character, and of "traditions" that a particular class might develop over the course of several reunions.[7] Nevertheless, a general shift in focus of the kind illustrated in the accompanying table, though inconclusive, cannot be dismissed as we try to understand the influence of lifecourse on high school reunion experiences. A much broader statistical analysis—far beyond the scope of the present study—would be required to confirm

TABLE I *Elements of Reunion Ritual*

	10TH YEAR	15TH YEAR	20TH YEAR	30TH YEAR	40TH YEAR	50TH YEAR
Ritual References to the Present	Most Children Most Eligible Woman Most Eligible Man Most Changed Least Changed New Class Clown Came the Farthest Most Changed Grayest	Male With the Longest Hair Longest Married First Time Newlyweds Farthest Traveled Most Children Newest Baby	Farthest Traveled Longest Married Most Children Boldest Shortest Distance Traveled We Didn't Believe You'd Come	Farthest Traveled Door Prizes Reading of the Class Résumé	Door Prizes	None
Ritual References to the Past			Showing of films and slides taken in high school	The Way We Were/Where We Are Today Outline of historic events since graduation	Reading of the Class Prophecy Reading of excerpts from the school newspaper Showing of photographs with opaque projector	None
Teachers Invited	No	No	Yes	Yes	Yes	Yes
Music	Contemporary	Contemporary	High school	High school	High school	High school
Place	Shopping mall	Ramada Inn	Barn owned by couple	Country club	Country club	Country club
Display of Memorabilia	No	No	No	Yes	Yes	No
Reference to history	No	No	No	Yes	Yes	No
Singing of School Song	No	No	No	Yes	Yes	No

the generality of this observation, but I am more convinced (and intrigued) by the accounts provided by my informants of their subjective experiences of reunions attended at different points in their lifecourses than I would be by masses of figures.

When I talked to members of the Class of '42 after their reunion, they unanimously asserted that this reunion was much more enjoyable than the one they held twenty years before. In speaking of the changing quality of their reunion experience, many informants summed up in the idiom of "mellowing" the sense of deepening maturity that emerged in their later reunion. For example:

It was not like this twenty years ago. I think at that time we were trying to impress each other. Maybe not consciously, we were all scared. And now we've gotten over that hump. It's like we get mellow with age or something.

We're more natural now. We know what we are now. Twenty years ago, we tried to dress a little more and impress each other a little more, but now we feel more at home with each other. I guess we mellow with age.

In high school, you have all kinds of association with people and feel that you like someone and don't like someone and so on, but so many aspects of that were submerged. Everyone was very mellow.

People were pretty mellow. [Unlike the twentieth-year reunion,] there was never any of the thinking back to high school days when "you did this and I did this": just warm, emotional meetings.

[In the twentieth-year reunion] there were some of them who were a little more stuck-up than they were at this one. And now people were much mellower. Everybody talked to everyone. I don't think I talked to half of them at the twentieth reunion.

What is interesting, however, is that the term "mellowing" is not used exclusively by older attendees. Younger reuniters used this term, too, in comparing the present reunion with one held in the past or with their experience of high school. Although the frequency with which the term is used increases with age, it appears as early as the tenth-year reunion.[8] In explaining why the twentieth-year reunion he had just attended was "a lot more fun," Mike Harrison, a member of the Elm High School Class of '62, put it this way:

> Maturity. Maturity, I think, maturity. Ten years out of high school, some of the families had young kids at the time and other hassles and problems, and now they're getting older, pretty much set on where they're going to be, and maybe [they have] more confidence in themselves, too. You see, maybe that's the reason. There were a lot of people who had matured quite a lot in the last ten years, you know—more mellow, no fights or anything. Like, "I whipped your butt ten years ago, and I could still do it." But years ago, everybody fought. I shouldn't say everyone, but you'd always see something going on. But now . . .

The range of meaning signified by the term "mellowing" is broad, but speaks to the essential elements of a specific manifestation of maturity that becomes increasingly evident in the ritual performance of reunions held later in life. On one level, mellowing occurs as a process of personal maturation: the crude high-school self is polished, its rough edges of competitiveness and insecurity are sloughed off, until a cultured (in the sense of having mastery over the symbol systems of his or her world), socially adept, self-aware, and confident individual emerges. On another level, mellowing speaks of the melting away of past interpersonal tensions and conflict, which are superseded by a sense of camaraderie and solidarity, and a mutual acknowledgment that—no matter what form relationships may have once taken—each class member is a precious link in the biography of the others.

The more general notion of maturity signifies the development and growth that occurs within the self. What is signified by the term mellowing, however, is a moving perspective on the relationship between self and others. Youth may prompt American individuals to identify that which separates them from others, and competition and comparison may be a natural part of this effort to know who they are vis-à-vis others. But the greater self-understanding that comes with age redirects them to find common ground with others, while at the same time allowing them to transcend the dictates of peer pressure, of conformity, and to enter into "freestanding friendship with those who shared [them]" in the formative years of their lives (Sheehy). The changing nature of American high school reunions seems to encode this idealistic vision of human maturity, in which the ultimate destination is freedom to draw toward—not away from—others.

6 Going Home: High School Reunions in American Adulthood

This had been the road of Destiny; had taken us to those early
accidents of fortune which predetermined for us all that we can ever
be. Now I understand that the same road was to bring us together
again. Whatever we had missed, we possessed together the precious,
the incommunicable past.

—*Willa Cather,* My Antonia

Many of the people I met at reunions told me the class reunion is a time
to reminisce about the adolescent past and "feel young again." But to
see the phenomenon of the high school reunion simply as an exercise in
nostalgia, a temporary manifestation of self-indulgent sentimentality
over "lost youth," would confine us to a rose-colored view and veil our
eyes to the anthropological significance of this unique ritual form.
Certainly class reunions *reunite* Americans with their youthful past and
with the people who helped create their remembrances of that past, but
it is what the past does in the present that makes reunions compelling.

At the core of my analysis of high school reunions are the phenomenological interplay between high school past and adult present in the
drama of human development, and the forming and re-forming of the
high school class as a community of memory in order to collectively
create meaning. In the high school reunion, Americans are (to paraphrase Fernandez) thrown into a room full of mirrors in which they
can see themselves (1986: 184). Through the arrangement of the light
and shadow of the high school self seen in classmates' memories, as well
as the silhouettes of adult classmates that have been drawn by inescapable life processes—biological, social, and historical—Americans seize

images of their present selves in relation to others and place their biographies in the context of the larger processes that embrace them. In the struggle over meaning that emerges in each high school reunion, Americans construct new symbols and stories uniquely fitted to their high school class as they participate in meaning-making activities as memory-bearing persons situated in specific historical and lifecourse positions. In the process, the high school reunion mediates individual meaning with collective meaning and enriches the individual biography with a sense of connection to culture and history.

As my ethnography of American high school reunions draws to a close, there remains one issue I have yet to discuss. The American high school reunions I studied sprung spontaneously from the initiative of individuals who were under no obligation to participate. What was the motivation? Is there anything special about this society that makes high school reunions compelling to Americans? By way of conclusion, I would like to explore the sociocultural setting that nurtures the motivation for high school reunions, and to examine the significance of reunions in American adulthood, focusing on the milieu in which people construct their "biographies of the self."

Semantic Solitude

"Each man must look to himself to teach him the meaning of life. It is not something discovered: it is something molded." This quote from Saint-Exupéry (1939: 48) points to the fundamental and universal task of adulthood. Meaning is not inherent in life, nor does it come automatically with experience. We have to mold the meaning of our lives in ways that account for our own congeries of particularities by seeking the connecting threads in the Story of My Life. We do so in the company of our contemporaries, using cultural symbols accessible to us in the historical contexts in which we find ourselves. An awareness of our own uniqueness, as well as our connection to others, to culture and to history, is essential to the well-being of the self. In constructing the biography of the self, we must reconcile the tension between our individuality and collectivity, because submission either to self-complacency on the one hand, or to conformity on the other, leads us to lose our sense of authenticity and uniqueness, our sense of having a foundation on which our self can be grounded. Adult persons every-where must seek this resonance between individual self and society in the moments of everyday social interaction, and abstract it into the meaning of their lives. But adulthood in postindustrial American society, as many scholars in adult development agree, is increasingly complex, ambiguous, and in constant flux.[1] The life-long task of constructing meaning has become enormously challenging.

The industrial revolution fundamentally changed the ways Americans engage in the social world, bringing mass longevity, changes in gender roles, and reorganization of the patterns of labor participation. It also brought about new ways to conceive of the course of life.[2] The development of various social institutions has divided the social world into many clearly demarcated life domains, each with its own goals and purposes. Separation of the private and public (e.g., family and work), as well as fragmentation in every level of the "public" world (e.g., education, business, politics), affects the ways Americans perceive and organize their personal lives. In a fragmented life-world, Americans may develop a sophisticated ability to deal with each sector of life, but since the relationships between the various sectors remain largely an abstraction, they find it difficult to grasp a sense of the lifecourse as an integrated whole.[3]

In order to help render tangible the individual sense of lifecourse, what has emerged in America is a collective struggle to construct the stories and narratives by which Americans can increase their sense of control over adulthood. In attempting to overcome ambiguities and possibly find a model that might work for their own lives, Americans read biographies and autobiographies of famous men and women, and turn to "expert" advice from various fields—newspaper columns, books, and self-help manuals written by psychologists, sociologists, medical doctors, and successful businesspeople. Taken together, these form a cultural discourse on the self and the lifecourse in which various narratives and symbols are developed and used to interpret personal events and experiences in adulthood. And yet this discourse is hardly woven into a seamless whole; its amorphous components often contradict one another,[4] as in the exhortation to age gracefully versus prescriptions for remaining young.

It has been argued that a holistic vision for the lifecourse is essential to adult development.[5] And yet, in a pluralized and fragmented life world, adult Americans must struggle to untangle various axes of time, modulating biological rhythm with the pace of institutional life, aligning such affective and instrumental realms of life as love and work and negotiating a reliable and harmonious balance between the various "life contours"—social, normative, occupational, psychological, material, physiological—to which they have access (Smelser 1980). They may listen to the changing language in which current ideals of selfhood are expressed, discern the separate strands of such discourse, and think about what those strands imply for their own life (Swidler 1980).

Moreover, as the world of information expands, there is a tendency for the immediate social circle in which Americans intimately participate to shrink. Age, class, occupation, ethnicity, and lifestyle preferences segregate social circles of individuals.[6] The vision of society beyond the intimate social circles in which Americans participate, and the roles that society, culture, and biology play in the lives of Americans at large, are only vaguely gleaned from secondhand images and information filtered through the mass media. Segregated in social circles of intimates and thus alienated from a vision of the whole, Americans may have, to borrow Berman's phrase, "missed or broken the connection between [their] culture and [their] lives" (1987: 24).

The popular reception of Gail Sheehy's best-selling *Passages: Predictable Crises of Adult Life* in the mid-1970's may be understood as an expression of the sense of urgency felt by many Americans as industrial America was coming to maturity. This book guided many Americans as they were struggling to render predictable a culturally unpredictable adulthood and to find connections between individual lives and societal lifecourse patterns. The model of adult life presented by Sheehy may have been illuminating to many American readers because it was built upon a uniquely American notion of selfhood. The language of the following statement from Sheehy's *Passages*, though reflecting the period in which it was written, encapsulates this cultural archetype.

> The most important words in midlife are: Let go. Let it happen to you. Let it happen to your partner. Let the feelings. Let the changes.
> You can take everything with you when you leave on the midlife

journey. You are moving away. Away from institutional claims and other people's agendas. Away from external evaluations and accreditations, in search of an inner validation. You are moving out of roles and into the self. If I could give everyone a gift for the send-off on this journey, it would be a tent. A tent for tentativeness. The gift of portable roots.

To reach the clearing beyond, we must stay with the weightless journey through uncertainty. Whatever counterfeit safety we hold over from investments in people and institutions must be given up. The inner custodian must be unseated from the controls. No foreign power can direct our journey from now on. It is for each of us to find a course that is valid by our own reckoning. (1977: 364)

In contrast to other societies in which the social engagement of the self is emphasized,[7] in the United States the emphasis is on the clearly bounded individual and the cultivation of his or her uniqueness through the maintenance of autonomy and freedom from outer forces.[8] The self-actualization that follows adolescence requires metaphysically breaking free from family, community, and past. To borrow a phrase from the authors of the now classic *Habits of the Heart*, "it is almost to give birth to oneself."[9] On the way to becoming a "successful" person, changes are not only expected but considered prerequisite for achievement and growth; and validations and justifications for such changes must come from nowhere other than the inner self. Moving on, going through changes, the American identity must be flexible, nesting in a tentative tent, carrying with it its portable roots. Fixity implies stagnation and the running dry of individual potential, and Americans often feel they must guard themselves against this perceived pitfall. Erikson, perhaps the most influential writer in shaping the American vision of the lifecourse, similarly observed:

> The process of American identity formation seems to support an individual's ego identity as long as he can preserve a certain element of deliberate tentativeness or autonomous choice. The individual must be able to convince himself that the next step is up to him and that no matter where he is staying or going he always has the choice of leaving or turning in the opposite direction if he chooses to do so. (1963: 286)

Emphasized in this culturally construed notion of self and lifecourse are autonomous choice and self-reliance, the cultivation of a unique self, and an open road for human potential. The self, in this view, is a lonely navigator manipulating and sometimes even striving against the currents of destiny as it steers toward its own future. This is the idea encoded in the perpetual American notions of "success" and "achievement," especially prevalent among those oriented toward upward mobility.

Needless to say, what I am describing here is not how Americans actually live, nor is it how every American actually thinks. Social class, gender, ethnicity, and occupational culture, as well as ideology, are important variables that affect the ways Americans actually think and act. And yet, while many—perhaps most—Americans may not live out or subscribe to this cultural vision, none need have it explained, so firmly is it rooted in this society's popular consciousness, and reiterated and perpetuated in all forms of cultural discourse. Though the discourse may only vaguely reflect reality, there is a "consensus discourse" in the United States about the self and its lifecourse.

This vision of the individual as isolated and wholly in charge of its own destiny is a cultural heritage identified by Alexis de Tocqueville a century and a half ago. But as the social and symbolic milieu of adulthood is increasingly differentiated, segregated, and destabilized, the cultural ideology of individualism poses problems. Tocqueville warned that the development of democratic individualism "disposes each member of the community to sever himself from the mass of his fellows and to draw apart with his family and his friends, so that after he has thus formed a little circle of his own, he willingly leaves society at large to itself. . . . [Democracy] throws him back forever upon himself alone and threatens in the end to confine him entirely within the solitude of his own heart" (1945: 2:104–6).

Many American critiques suggest that such a trend is indeed under way in American society today.[10] On the basis of two large-scale national surveys conducted some twenty years apart, Veroff, Douvan, and Kulka documented that the locus of meaning is shifting more and more away from society and toward the individual.[11] This tendency of turning away from social relations as the base of self definition is particularly pronounced among the more educated, and tends to result in a more individuated, personalized kind of self-integration.

American cultural idioms of autonomy and self-reliance may support the individual's freedom to retreat into a small social circle and be content in the meaning he or she constructs therein. But these cultural idioms define personality, achievement, and the purpose of human life in ways that leave individuals isolated within these circles of meaning. Veroff and his colleagues found that Americans "felt better about themselves than twenty years earlier because they were more likely to judge themselves less by general rules or standards, and feel less fault in falling short of the normative moral mark. But as social roles and practice lose their moral coherence, Americans experience more doubt about who they 'really' are and more difficulty in finding an authentic self. Thus, over time, guilt declines but anxiety increases."[12]

The cultural rhetoric of success and personal growth emphasizes the openness of possibilities but does not define their limitations, nor does it offer overarching and integrated standards by which people can evaluate their own success. In contrast to other societies—such as Japan, to some extent—where the status of the individual is largely defined by group membership and position within a group, the significant unit in the American status system is "the individual, unfettered by family, or other group affiliation, afforded equality of opportunity to make himself into the 'best' expression he can of the most valued characteristics of the society": "Just as an individual's position on the scale of rank is not determined by ascribed characteristics, that is, by his intrinsic qualities, so there are no fixed standards of behavior which serve to mark status. The only clearly defined cultural standards against which status can be measured are the gross standards of income, consumption, and conformity to rational procedures for attaining ends" (Schneider and Smith 1973: 24).

The social milieu of contemporary American adulthood cuts off individual efforts at making sense and the personal universe of meaning from the larger society and places them in semantic solitude. The meaning Americans construct in this semantic solitude is fragile, and its authenticity uncertain. If the little universe of meaning one constructs around oneself becomes the principal or only source of validation available, how then can one be assured of the authenticity of the meaning constructed (Bellah et al. 1985)? In sorting out the multiplicity of possible career options in adult life, meaning seems to a large degree negotiable. This may be why American minds are "peculiarly reflexive" (P. Berger, B. Berger, and Kellner 1973). But it is not an easy task for many Americans, to paraphrase Giele (1980), to negotiate meaning in a way that extends beyond the idiosyncratic and has some socially shared value. The importance of maintaining a resonance between individual meaning and social meaning is paramount, for at the extremes of semantic individualism lie the danger of moving away from inner conviction into the culture of conformity and the danger of moving away from others into a "culture of narcissism."[13]

Just as overarching generalizations involve risks, so do cross-cultural comparisons. Nevertheless, some comments comparing the United States with my native Japan may help us better understand the American case. It is my impression that even though Japan, too, is a "culture of becoming," where ideas of individual choice and achievement have become firmly rooted in popular consciousness, and even though industrialization has brought changes in adulthood similar to those in the United States, the individual Japanese self and its biography have not been cut off from those of others in the way they have been in the United States. Rather, it has been said that the Japanese conceive of the individual as being connected to others, and are characterized as making firmer commitments to the roles associated with one's position in society.[14] Thus, it is not difficult to imagine that the ways in which the problems of adulthood take expression and are dealt with differ in the two countries. To validate this impression would require more empirical studies focusing on comparative adulthood.[15] One thing I can say with a certain amount of conviction, however, is that the fragmentation of the social world has drawn the Japanese into ever more complicated webs of social relationships.

Of particular relevance to the discussion at hand are the different roles high schools play in the cultural biographies of Americans and Japanese, a subject I touched on in Chapter 1. In Japan, the development of institutional occupations has differentiated various career tracks, and the track one chooses during the high school entrance examination process largely determines one's future career.[16] Thus, differentiation increases awareness of the position of the self. Rohlen observes:

> High school entrance exams then sort each age cohort into what amounts to an eight- to ten-tier high school ranking system. Future occupational and status levels [elite managerial, blue-collar, and so forth] are closely equated to this ranking. Further, at the point of high school entrance the entire age cohort is divided into three largely immutable classificatory distinctions: those leaving school, those entering vocational ranks, and those going on to academic high schools. In Japan's cities, 95 percent of all students are advancing to high school and nearly as many are graduating, signifying the near demise of the high school degree as a mark of distinction. The type of high school and the status of one's university are the crucial measures.
>
> At the end of high school, differentiation occurs once more. About half of the nation's young men are ranked at that time according to the calibration of university stature. Their future employment and social identity will be significantly influenced by which university they attend. From high school on, Japanese experience a progressively sharper differentiation and hierarchy within generations. One's awareness of one's place in a larger social world increases, and with the approaching entry to adult society, competition intensifies and opportunities narrow. (1983: 308, 310)

The results of a cross-cultural survey conducted by a Tokyo-based research firm regarding the aspirations of American and Japanese high school students are inconclusive but interesting testimony to the fact that, by the time they graduate from high school, Japanese students have a rather realistic vision of their future.[17] Whereas 47 percent of the American students surveyed said they hope to become lawyers, doctors, professors, or other professionals, 46 percent of their Japanese counterparts foresaw working in a small or medium-size firm by the time they are in their thirties, 32 percent envisioned working in a large corporation, 28 percent said they would work as engineers, translators, or in other technical jobs, and 27 percent said they would probably become civil servants. It would seem that, while Japanese high schools promote an awareness of limitations, American high schools perpetuate the American ideal of individual possibility.[18]

Of course, this does not mean that the Japanese lifecourse is orderly and devoid of ambiguities and conflicts.[19] In fact, mass longevity and changes in gender roles are radically affecting the way Japanese conceptualize the lifecourse. The once taken-for-granted notion of lifetime employment, for instance, has been shown to be contradicted by statistical reality. Rose Coser, speaking of the United States, writes that, "In modern society it becomes increasingly difficult for a young person to know what kind of adult he will become, because the goals of adult status can hardly be formulated until after a period of general preparation and experimentation" (1969: 105). In Japan, too, despite the overwhelming power of high school to place students in various career tracks that have lifelong implications, there is no lack of ambiguity, uncertainty, or change. Nonetheless, students tend to form a vision of the future that is not divorced from reality. Their American counterparts, in contrast, feel that their life careers are relatively open, despite the undeniable existence of many factors that are beyond individual control and may affect their social achievement.

In Search of the Whole

In life after high school, Americans pass through an ever-changing kaleidoscope of social experiences. They struggle within a small universe of meaning to achieve integration in a distinctive style, to generate a sense of continuity of self, and to plan for a meaningful future. They may crave a vision of human life that transcends individual experiences yet simultaneously provides a framework for understanding their own experiences, for interpreting their positions in society and their own progress as whole persons. But such a vision is fragmented and abstract. Nevertheless, finding a frame of significance to relate their isolated experiences to those of others and to society at large is essential if they are to invest their biographies with richness and depth.

Such frames of significance may be elusive as Americans drift through the prosaic rounds of everyday life. In her study of former workers at the Amoskeag Mills in Manchester, New Hampshire, Tamara Hareven found that her informants showed tremendous difficulty in recalling and relating their experience of being workers at the old mill (shut down in 1932) until they saw an exhibit at a local art gallery describing the historical changes that affected the architectural landscape and lives in Amoskeag (1978). Only when an identification of the connection between isolated experience and collective historical processes was established through this public display were their memories stimulated and the historical significance of their working lives began to take clear shape in their life stories. Hareven points out that for most Americans, "such links are exceedingly difficult to identify unless the individuals participated in a common distinct cultural activity, organization or group with a shared interest, or if their lives were affected directly by a common dramatic event, [such as] a labor movement, or a strike, or . . . an organized political or social activity" (p. 143).

This may be one reason why the actual staging of a reunion is important. As we have seen, the moment of receiving a reunion invitation (or deciding to organize an event) inspired thoughts about high school, even if the recipient did not think much about it in everyday life. In bringing former classmates together for a live ritual performance, the reunion compels individuals to reidentify with their membership in their old class and focus their attention on their lives since high school. Through the telling of individual and collective experiences, this ritual performance establishes links that are only dimly perceived in everyday life. In Chapter 3, I discussed the way historical and lifecourse consciousnesses are brought together in the creation of the tenth-year reunion of the Class of '72. In Chapter 4, we saw in two life stories various ways in which the past interacts with the present in the individual construction of meaning. In Chapter 5, through a description of the fortieth-year reunion of the Class of '42, I examined how reunions reconstruct the meaning of high school experience, how the participant is reconnected to the community of memory that is the high school cohort, and how the relationship between the participant and that community can change during the lifecourse. High school reunions foster moments of reflexivity that allow individual biographies to be grounded, authenticated, confirmed, and even changed.

Certainly this power of relating and linking the individual with the group and its history, or of fostering reflexivity, is not unique to the high school reunion. Rather, it is a role inherent in collective performance. Barbara Myerhoff's study of what she calls a "nonce ritual" staged by Jewish senior citizens is a wonderful example of how, through collective performance, people generate a sense of connection to the past, to history and cultural heritage, and confirm the significance of their lives (1977).[20] No doubt there are many such rituals in various sectors of American society, such as ethnic, religious, occupational, and gay and lesbian communities. However, unlike collective performances that occur in narrower sectors of American society in which membership is limited to those who share a certain trait, membership in the community of memory formed by former public high school classmates is far more encompassing of the American population. As one informant remarked, "high school reunions are something that are supposed to happen sooner or later to everyone," regardless of social class, ethnicity, or occupation; the only prerequisite is having gone to a public high school. Considering that today more than 90 percent of Americans attend high school, I cannot think of another ritual occasion more fitted to be called a "tribal rite" of the postindustrial United States.

And yet, the number of people who are eligible to attend is not the only factor that makes this ritual uniquely important in American adulthood. Its importance is derived from the distinctive characteristics of the school class cohort and the unique position it occupies in American lifecourse.

In contrast to Japan, where individual school populations are homogenized by a selective admission process, in most parts of the United States public high school classes are composed of students from diverse sociocultural backgrounds. It is like a society in miniature, reflecting the social organization of the community that the high school serves. But once graduates leave high school, they immediately begin to build the narrower, personal communities that will characterize their adulthood.

The high school reunion reconstructs that lost "society in miniature," but this time, diversity arises from the varying adult lives molded during the period of separation. One informant commented that attending his reunion "was a dazzling experience. I have never seen so many different types of people at once. We had farmers and businessmen, lawyers and doctors, and some Ph.D.'s. Some were divorced, some already retired, some recently remarried." The M.C. of the thirtieth-year reunion of the Elm High Class of '52 may have been exaggerating when he suggested that participants were so diverse "we could build our own town." Nevertheless, by throwing together people from all walks of life who are all going through different experiences at the time of the reunion, the reunion provides participants with a rare opportunity to see firsthand (as one informant put it) "what's going on among the people of my age in the society at large." The particular configuration of lifecourses that emerges in the high school reunion is far more representative of the larger society than those readily available in practically any other social setting.

As important as this diversity are the things members of a high school class have in common. Whatever the lifestyle that classmates lead today, they have in common the same historical position, the same lifecourse position, and the same geographical point of departure from which they embarked on their journey to adult life.

"To gauge my life" was one of the most common reasons people offered for attending reunions. A local newspaper in Champaign-Urbana used this phrase in a headline for an article on local class reunions.[21] For any comparison to be effective, it must be based on one or more common denominators, and the high school reunion, by providing these points of commonality, makes the comparisons that occur at reunions more persuasive than those in just about any other context; the fact that participants knew one another during their formative years makes the comparisons all the more compelling and convincing. That the comparisons that occur between former classmates are *controlled comparisons* makes it easier to assign significance to parallels and differences, to continuities and changes.

As I argued earlier, American cultural idioms of personhood point the way to openness and freedom, but fail to define the limits of personal growth or achievement. At each reunion, the collectively constructed Story of Our Class charts the array of life trajectories of the high school cohort. It illustrates how far classmates have gone in life having started from the same place, having lived through the same historical events, and having reached the same stage in biological development. By presenting a compendium of lives in the same high school cohort, the story gives concrete shape to participants' visions of human possibility, replacing at least temporarily the nebulous images offered elsewhere, and participants use this directory to try to locate their lives vis-à-vis others in their class.

Moreover, the high school cohort differs in important ways from the generic age cohort. An age cohort is composed of individuals who share *abstract* memories of historical events (Hochschild 1978, Matthews 1986). A high school cohort, by contrast, shares concrete memories of being in the same high school during the same years, of certain dramas of interpersonal interaction, of the youthful struggle of the identity game. They remember not only the historical events that affected their school days, but also what Sarah Matthews calls the "historical self": who you and they were in the days in which friendship or enmity was established (1986: 148). They are powerful witnesses to continuity and to change in one's self since high school, and are able to verify and authorize them in a way that friends made later in life cannot.

Thus, the various assessments of lives that take place at reunions are not based on one criterion, but are holistic, involving various axes of comparison, such as family, work, and body, as well as personal and interpersonal maturity. (For example, "Little Sally, who was so shy in school, is now a dependable office worker, mother of three, and better looking than any of the women in our cheerleading squad.") Such a coherent assessment may be hard to obtain in other institutional settings or in the personal communities Americans construct for themselves. Further, while the information on aging and lifecourse provided by specialists, experts, and the mass media tends to focus on one dimension of a person and is not integrated into a coherent whole, a high school reunion can put the pieces of the fragmented self back together, and thus provides an opportunity for a total evaluation of the self and its trajectory. Because people trace their life trajectory from high school at high school reunions, the basic reference point for evaluation is always high school experience, and thus the idiom of "mellowing"—an alternative to more general and familiar cultural concepts of maturing—is generated in the reunion discourse to assess the evolution of the self since high school; the crude, inchoate high school self is seen to be smoothed into a well-rounded person with distinctive individuality.

In youth, schools like Elm High School formed a coherent moral community that was integral to the development of adolescent self-awareness. It was the undeniable reality that students had to deal with in their present-tense relationships with classmates. It often demanded commitment and the devotion of the entire self. The community of memory that forms and re-forms in the reunion, by contrast, characteristically lacks such a sharing of the here-and-now of life, and thus lacks the power of collective coercion that could affect one's present life. Though membership is predefined, one is free to determine the importance of that membership in one's present life. The reunion guarantees a safe, temporary, and special context for life evaluations, separated from the past as well as the institutional communities to which one now belongs. Meaning constructed in the reunion is not coercive, like that handed down by other communities of meaning such as religious or occupational communities, but rather is like a souvenir that one can take home and use (or ignore) to suit to one's own biographical needs.

As we have seen, a discussion of the relationship between the socio-cultural milieu of American adulthood and high school reunions puts in perspective the importance of this collective performance. Simply put: *The high school reunion is a rare and provocative occasion available to almost all American men and women that enables them to step outside their semantic solitude and participate in the collective construction of meaning by which they interpret, assess, and authenticate their own unfolding biographies.* Through the sense-making activities they engage in with other members of their class, they gain a vision of the wider societal patterns of the lifecourse, and create symbols and narratives for understanding life that give concrete shape to culturally obscure notions of personal growth, success, and maturity in a way most fitted to their changing life situations. The meaning constructed in reunions is more concrete, holistic, and convincing than that created in perhaps any other setting available to American adults, and this meaning releases participants, at least temporarily, from ambiguity and painful wrestling with conventional values as they struggle to become whomever they may be.

It seems that people everywhere need "traveling companions" to help direct, measure, and validate their lifelong biographical development. It seems also that the people with whom one went through the intense and critical transition that occurs on the threshold of adulthood are likely to be the best companions. It has been reported that in certain tribal societies, an age cohort that went through puberty rites at the same time keeps in contact throughout adulthood and forms a lifelong reference group for individual social comparison. The Gusii of Kenya studied by Robert LeVine measure their progress and stagnation "invidiously against that of a visible [age cohort] rather than measuring it against an abstract concept of the ideal life stages" (1980: 92). In industrial America, the high school cohort—a community of memory originating in an educational institution—not only forms a reference group for comparison, but more significantly forms a community of meaning, or, to borrow Plath's phrase, a lifelong "convoy" that gets together once in a while to collectively guard individual biographies from a loss of vision, direction, and significance.

The high school reunion may also be the most appropriate ritual for people experiencing adulthood in industrial and postindustrial American society. In a fragmented social world, Americans belong to many institutional communities, each demanding a distinctive style of commitment, each demanding adjustment to its own pace, but none of which are holistic. There remains "the urge of the soul for a vision of itself, in its entirety" (Myerhoff and Metzger 1980: 98). Americans need vision for human potential and limitation, need guidelines that are not idiosyncratic but have some socially shared meaning that can symbolize the transformations a person will undergo throughout the lifecourse. Many scholars in human development lament the lack of rites of passage in adulthood, but even if they did exist, off-the-rack rites that move people mechanically from one stage of the lifecourse to the next would be of little practical use in contemporary American society. Instead of rituals that express and teach cultural norms of how to live and how to give life meaning, perhaps what are more useful (or desirable) are spontaneous performances, custom-made to fit the current biographical needs of participants, rites that put the capacity to make meaning into the hands of participants, and can best serve the American's changing perspectives in adulthood.

Uncovering "Reunions"

A popular view of rituals holds that traditional rituals are irreconcilable with modern society, and that they decrease in number and vitality as a society industrializes. In contrast, my findings on high school reunions in the United States imply that in the case of the reunion, the reverse may be true. Since the reunion as a ritual form presupposes separation, spatial mobility and discontinuity of life experience are minimal preconditions for such a performance. That is, as a society becomes more industrialized, the social world becomes more segmented, and intercommunity mobility becomes inevitable, the impetus for reunions might logically increase. Simply stated, the reunion thrives when the community is dispersed.

As industrialization and modernization sweep over most of the world, migration and mobility are becoming commonplace social conditions embracing much of the human population. The modern life-course is characterized by successive moves from one demarcated social or institutional experience to another. It may be that "reunion-like" phenomena are occurring in unexpected contexts, taking different names and forms (e.g., a pilgrimage to a cultural or historical Mecca).[22] Events we know as a communal festival or traditional ceremony, though not bearing the name "reunion," may well serve that role, providing an occasion to bring back those who have left the community and reunite them with their physical and metaphysical homes.

For example, the Fighting Festival I studied in Himeji, Japan (Ikeda 1990), is becoming more vigorous as the community's boundaries become more and more blurred in the face of an encroaching industrial order. I observed that the real power of this community festival in post-industrial Japan is to bring back those who have moved outside the festival community, and to produce and reproduce a symbolic community, bounded by the festival, that lends a sense of significance to their lives.

A more direct and telling case is the resurgence of the *tugu* ceremony (the construction of ancestral tombs and ritual activities associated with it) among the Toba Batak in Indonesia, studied by Edward Bruner (1987). He finds that within a decade after extensive migration began, the Batak who had migrated and established themselves in urban communities revived this ceremony and built megalithic monuments on their ancestral homelands. The *tugu* ceremony brings back the dispersed members of the clan, reunites them with the home they left and with an earlier phase of their own as well as their family's historical experience. In Bruner's words:

[The *tugu* ritual] connects what you are with what you were. It is a way to recapture the past, indeed, to return to it, so as to bridge the felt discrepancy between discourse and experience. Through the *tugu* ritual the urbanite has an opportunity to witness a representation of his historical self, to reflect upon his essential Batakness, and to journey back in time to a former phase of his cultural life. It is a generative and regenerative experience, for with the construction of the *tugu*, as a representation of the clan ancestor, the Batak construct themselves, align the past with the present, the rural with the urban, the moral with the material. (1987: 148)

It would be a mistake to interpret these performances of "tradition" or "the past" as indicating collective indulgence in nostalgia, stagnant imaginations, or simple traditionalism. Rather, we have to understand the creative processes whereby the past is used as a resource in responding to the current conditions in which persons find themselves (Bestor 1989). In the struggle to interpret our present condition, Anthony Cohen writes, "We use our past experience to render stimuli into a form sufficiently familiar that we can attach some sense to them. Our experience functions as what Geertz called a model of reality. Without such models we should have no basis from which to orient ourselves to the phenomenon requiring interpretation" (1985: 99).

"Home," therefore, for the members of modern, industrialized societies, is not necessarily the geographical location where one is born and grows up. Home can be any earlier period of one's life or earlier experience, if it is infused with meaning and felt to be the core of one's biography. Some of the Americans who spoke to me during the course of my study found home in some place or time other than high school and late adolescence. Some may discover their high school home in their later years, as in the case of the many men and women whose fiftieth-year reunion was the first they had attended. Nevertheless, I would contend that the public high school experience in America is so nearly universal, and so homogenous in critical respects, that its attraction as a home is unique, and uniquely powerful. Returning home, in this broad definition, is the essence of the reunion.

The study of "reunion-like" phenomena, such as the Fighting Festival and the *tugu* ceremony, will surely become increasingly significant as the industrial social order spreads to more and more societies, and penetrates more deeply in those where it has already been established. In a modern society such as the United States, Myerhoff and Metzger write, "increasingly we find ourselves, individually and collectively, inventing our own symbols and rituals, for if the opportunities for understanding the human condition through myth and ritual have diminished, the necessity and desire for them have not lessened" (1980: 97). To deepen our understanding of such developments, we must go beyond the study of ritual as a closed system of symbols and meanings, a discrete text divorced from real people and sociocultural and historical context, and study such performances in relation to the settings that nurture them. For the modern man and woman, home is where the heart wants to be. The task of the anthropologist is to discover those homes and examine the importance of returning there.

Reference Matter

NOTES

CHAPTER ONE

1. Brown suggests that the reunions of more "sophisticated urban
    high schools" follow the patterns of what he terms "mass culture"
    rituals, while the reunions of smaller, more rural high schools fol-
    low the patterns of folklore culture. But he does not substantiate
    this point in his essay (1985: 107–13). Humphrey and Humphrey
    describe the class reunion they attended as a "traditional festival"
    (1985: 99–106).
2. See White 1966: 1; Goodman 1979: 3; Plath 1983: 226.
3. In Japanese class reunions (*dōsōkai*), there are usually no formal
    ceremonial events such as the kind of award-giving ceremonies I
    describe in subsequent chapters; rather, it is an informal gathering
    in which former classmates rekindle old friendships over food and
    (sometimes) drinks. In some cases, an organized event may be
    planned, but this is rare and not as stylized as its American coun-
    terpart. In addition, one major uniqueness of the *dōsōkai* is that
    it is a formal organization associated with the school. When used
    to refer to class reunions, *dōsōkai* means literally "same-window
    gathering," but it also means "same-window *club*," referring to an
    organization that is akin to the American alumni association, and

its membership includes all the graduates of the school throughout its history. The presidency of such an association is a prestigious position, and these clubs sometimes exercise power over school administration and educational policy. Although in the United States alumni associations are common in universities and colleges, and probably some private high schools, too, the public high schools I studied do not have this type of formal organization.

4. See, among others, R. Mead 1973; Keyes 1976; Markey 1984; Lamb and Reeder 1986.

5. I should make it clear here that while my analysis of American society is of course informed by the classic *Habits of the Heart*, I use the term "community of memory" in a different sense than do Bellah et al. In their usage, a "community of memory" is a "genuine" community, in the sense that it has a history and does not forget that history. Their definition would include ethnic, racial, religious, and national communities. I use the term to denote a community that once existed, at an earlier point in an individual's lifecourse, but has since ceased to exist except as a memory.

6. Reinhardt 1966; *Digest of Education Statistics* (National Center for Education Statistics 1987).

7. These statistics were taken from Inagaki (1986: 77).

8. *Monbushō tōkei yōran* (Ministry of Education Statistical Handbook, Japanese Ministry of Education, 1996). The figure of 96 percent was calculated on the basis of the information in the tables on pp. 57 and 65, which show the number of students enrolled and the number actually graduated. Interestingly, the Japanese do not seem to be concerned with the rate of graduation.

9. For a more detailed description of the development of the Japanese high school, see Rohlen 1983.

10. Conant 1959; Coleman et al. 1974.

11. The Japanese system of secondary education is referred to in this section only for the purpose of elucidating the cultural uniqueness of the American high school as seen from a Japanese point of view. For the reader who is interested in more information, overviews of today's Japanese school system can be obtained from *Japanese Education Today: A Report from the Study of Education in Japan* (U.S. Department of Education 1987), and "School Education: Its History and Contemporary Status" (Inagaki 1986). The most compre-

hensive ethnography of the Japanese high school produced by an American anthropologist is *Japan's High Schools* (Rohlen 1983). Since his American perspective is instructive in understanding cross-cultural differences between high schools in Japan and American high schools, and since he studied high schools in the area where I grew up, I will refer to his observations of the Japanese high school to contrast with my Japanese perspective on the American high school.

12. Coleman et al. 1974; U.S. Department of Education 1987.

13. The association of equal education and free competition originates in efforts of the Meiji government (1868–1911) to replace the feudal class system with a competitive system based on merit rather than social class or origin. The basic ideology of Meiji educational reform was that anyone who excels academically can become a leader of the nation. Of course, in reality, only those who were unburdened by family responsibilities were able to devote themselves to academic study. Nevertheless, the Meiji reforms led to the social reorganization of Japanese society. Today, with the dramatic expansion of the middle class, the pressure to "get ahead" is enormous. A popular slogan is "Start earlier and study longer"; the competition starts as early as elementary school and students spend after-school hours in *juku* (private institutions that offer intensive preparation for entrance examinations). Students who "excel" tend to have parents who are well informed and can afford the cost of extra education. Consequently, there is more class homogeneity within a Japanese high school than is the case in American public schools.

14. 1983: 194. For the subculture of Japanese teenagers outside of school, see Merry White (1993).

15. See Lynd and Lynd 1956; Parsons 1959; Coleman 1961: 65; Friedenberg 1965; Schwartz and Merten 1967; Hill 1974.

16. Coleman 1961, 1965; Schwartz and Merton 1967; Eckert 1989.

17. The anthropologist Chris Kiefer characterizes "examination hell" as a puberty rite that serves to anchor the Japanese youth in a specific group. He argues that it serves to facilitate what he calls "conversion-through-suffering" (1974: 72), by which the Japanese learn the attitudes appropriate to specific roles in bureaucratic organizations, and by which they extend the emotional habits learned in the family to their age-mates.

18. "Rejected Cheerleaders Grow Up to be Erma and Johnny Carsons." From *At Wit's End*, a syndicated newspaper column by Erma Bombeck (*News Gazette*, Champaign, Ill., March 14, 1982).

19. Keyes 1976: 37–39: For the interested readers, the answers are: (1) b, (2) c, (3) c.

20. Biff's turning point comes when he discovers that the role model he has believed in—his father, who has been the most outspoken supporter of Biff's high school achievement—is a "fake." At this point Biff's high school glory becomes a sandcastle, and hopes for the future that were built on that sandcastle become meaningless.

21. This conversation is reconstructed from notes I took while viewing the program and is not a verbatim quote.

22. This episode was cited in Keyes 1976: 56–60.

23. June 1983. Markey expanded on this magazine article and published a book, *How to Survive Your High School Reunion and Other Midlife Crises* in 1984. The list of instructions is adapted from her book.

24. Chieko Mulhern 1984, personal communication.

25. As quoted in Basso 1984: 51.

26. Peacock 1984; Myerhoff 1978; R. Rosaldo 1986; Clifford 1986; Bruner 1984, 1986; Plath 1980; Marcus and Fischer 1986; Wolf 1992.

27. See Kirschner for her criticism of Geertzian interpretation (1987).

28. I.e., Kluckhohn's "comprehensive life story" (1945).

29. For example, Watson (1985) suggested that we take the hermeneutic textual approach, in which the ethnographer assumes a dialectical relationship with his subject. Frank (1979) stresses that the life story is a form that emerges in interactive discourse. Tilton (1980) notes that a life story is a construction derived from an enactment in a particular situation. Agar (1980: 223) defines life history as "an elaborate connected piece of talk presented in a social situation consisting of an informant and an ethnographer." Myerhoff (1980) saw life history as guided reflections through which informants try to make sense of their lives. Bruner (1984: 7) warns us not to fail to recognize the distinction between "a life as lived," "a life as experienced," and "a life as told"; a "life as told" is a narrative, "influenced by the cultural conventions of telling, by the audience, and by the social context."

30. Occasionally, interviewees specifically requested that certain statements remain confidential, or they said, "Don't tell anybody in my

class, but . . ." Although such material was usually poignantly relevant to my research, I have not included this kind of information in the life stories that appear in Chapters 3, 4, and 5.

31. All the names of persons, schools, and places as well as other identifying details have been changed in order to protect the privacy of interviewees. However, what people do and where they live reveal a lot about their life stories. In fact, occupation and residency are often used as significant symbols for self-awareness. I did my best to find cultural equivalents.

CHAPTER TWO

1. Hebb 1949; Paul 1959, 1967.
2. Sameroff and Chandler 1975; Paris and Lindauer 1977; Riegel 1977.
3. See also Bateson 1972; Goffman 1974.

CHAPTER THREE

1. Although it is customary to invite spouses of classmates to a reunion, I commonly found that spouses look out of place as their mates sit chatting with former classmates. Spouses frequently say later that they felt left out. Anticipating this, some participants do not bring their spouse along, fearing that he or she will not enjoy the event.

2. In studying a particular kind of ritual (wedding, healing ritual, etc.), ethnographers tend to provide a standardized account as the basis of their analysis, perhaps because of the anthropologist's preoccupation with cultural meaning. Further, because of the emphasis placed on the analysis of symbols and symbolic actions, the individuals who carry out the ritual tend to be reduced to "actors" or "performers" in the ethnographer's account. I am arguing against this tendency in the anthropological study of rituals.

3. In discussing the capacity of reunions to construct meaning, I will use Victor Turner's term "re-membering." Barbara Myerhoff explains how the hyphenated form differs from ordinary recollection as follows: "Re-membering is the reaggregation of one's members, the figures who properly belong to one's life story, one's own prior selves, the significant others without which the story cannot be completed" (Myerhoff 1984: 320).

4. Compare this with most American universities and colleges, which have an alumni office, or many Japanese high schools, in which the *dōsōkai* is a formal school institution that maintains contact with alumni (see Chap. 1, n. 3). One of the important functions of the *dōsōkai* as well as the alumni association of the American university or college is to solicit financial support from alumni for their "old school." Many private high schools in America have similar in-stitutionalized means of organizing alumni, but the public schools I studied usually do not.

5. One exceptional case is a high school class from a small rural town in the vicinity of Champaign-Urbana, which had been having their reunion every year for the fifty years since graduation. Class members whom I interviewed stressed that they feel their high school class is as close as a family and take pride in the class tradition that they established, knowing that no other class at their high school has such frequent reunions.

6. There is, however, a couple in Skokie, Illinois, who founded Class Reunion, Inc. in 1983. Their services range from tracking down miss-ing classmates, sending invitations, arranging events, providing re-union memorabilia (e.g., T-shirts) to giving counseling (*Wall Street Journal*, Aug. 17, 1983; *Austin American Statesman*, July 17, 1984).

CHAPTER FOUR

1. Note that Mary's perception, or at least her presentation, of herself is very different. In the previous chapter, Mary is quoted as saying that while "there were definite cliques" in high school, she "wasn't in any of them."

2. The notion of "staging a character"—that is, presenting an image with the aim of eliciting confirmation from others of a desired self-identity—comes from Goffman (1959: 252).

CHAPTER FIVE

1. It has been pointed out that Americans tend to avoid talking about social class in direct terms (Fussell 1983; Halle 1984; Linde 1987; Odendahl 1990; Ortner 1991; DeMott 1992). The Elm High School alumni whom I interviewed used the distinction between

the "university kids" and the "rest of the students" as an idiom for talking about socioeconomic class. Thus the "university kids" rubric includes children of wealthy families not necessarily connected to the university, who tended to join the clique formed by the children whose families were connected to the university.

2. The social structure of high school as described here by my informants from the Class of '42 is strikingly similar across the different Elm High School classes that I studied. First, the most comprehensive distinction is drawn in terms of socioeconomic class, with the "university kids" as a stand-in for "upper" or "upper-middle class." The second most comprehensive distinction involves the degree of participation in extracurricular activities. The location of residence ("town kids" versus "farm kids") was an objective factor influencing the degree of participation in after-school and social activities; the greater distances involved made it much more difficult for "farm kids" to participate in such activities. Personal qualities of the students, such as physical appearance and having (or not having) tact, can move the students up or down the high school social ladder. Academic ability, a critical factor in the lives of Japanese high school students, does not seem a decisive criterion in the formation of social structure in American high schools.

3. Incidentally, most of the items in the questionnaire prepared by the committee—such as education, work, and location of residence, as well as lifestyle questions about travel, hobbies, and organization membership—correspond to the major criteria that Americans use to judge a person's social standing, as described by Coleman and Rainwater in *Social Standing in America* (1978).

4. The class prophecy (along with the class will, in which seniors each name a particular underclassman to whom they bequeath their idiosyncratic talent) is a popular practice in high school yearbooks, especially among older Americans. Looking through yearbooks of Elm High School stored in the city library archive, I found that this practice began to appear in the yearbooks of the early thirties and waned in popularity beginning in the early sixties.

5. The reference, as many American readers probably recognize, is to the old history program, *You Are There,* hosted by Walter Cronkite.

6. Although gender is an important factor in generating different historical experience, Mrs. Thompson's case is by no means representative of the experience of the women of the Class of '42. To be sure, women did not generally experience the war as directly as men did, but rather vicariously, through their brothers, relatives, and boyfriends. Many had to make adjustments to their life paths (such as the timing of marriage), more women attended college than men for the first time in American history, and the war sent many women to work outside the home. But many returned to their traditional roles in response to the national postwar call for women to return to the home and turn the workplace back over to the men. Mrs. Thompson pinpointed without hesitation her college years as her best, but many of the women I interviewed (including those who went to college) identified high school as the best time of their lives.

7. One example of the last is the Class of '62's tradition of having a different theme for each reunion: Hawaiian for the tenth year, Western for the twentieth. It may be that by having members and their spouses dress in thematic costumes, the Class of '62 avoids the kind of competition-through-clothing that characterized earlier reunions.

8. See Mary's remark in Chapter 3, p. 69.

CHAPTER SIX

1. See, for example, Neugarten 1968; Neugarten and Datan 1973; Smelser and Erikson 1980.

2. According to Smelser, the modern definition of adolescence came into existence "when the years between twelve and eighteen became ambiguous—after the family had lost its control over the courtship, marriage, and economic training of the young, after apprenticeship as the typical initiation into adult work roles became weak, after the factory came to be regarded as an unsatisfactory if not evil place for young people, and before age-graded secondary schools arose as the principal vehicle for organizing those years" (1980: 2). See also Demos and Demos 1969; Demos 1978; Kett 1977. Adulthood, too, has become problematized in response to new currents generated by a changing industrial order. Accord-

ing to Jordan, adulthood, as we ordinarily think of it today, is largely an artifact of twentieth-century American culture (1976: 1). He suggests that the "discovery of adulthood" was later than that of adolescence, and was prompted by altered social conditions largely as a consequence of industrialization. Since the 1950's, scholarly and popular interest in adulthood has been growing (Giele 1980). Erikson and Smelser wondered at "this curiosity which has rather suddenly focused on adulthood as a developmental phase, when, in the past, we all wrote and read about childhood and adolescence" (Smelser and Erikson 1980: v). Today, as mass longevity spreads apace, we are starting to problematize old age by dividing this stage of life between the "young old" and the "old old."

3. On the complexity of American adulthood in the context of the fragmented social world that emerged with industrialization, see P. Berger, B. Berger, and Kellner 1973; Smelser and Erikson 1980; and Bellah et al. 1985. Pearlin talks about the "rearrangement of priorities" as an important strategy of modern men and women for maintaining their sense of well-being (1980).

4. Smelser and Erikson 1980; Bellah et al. 1985.

5. Neugarten is one of the strongest advocates of this viewpoint. She put it this way: "The individual is said to create a sense of self very early in life. . . . But it is perhaps not until adulthood that the individual creates a sense of the life-cycle; that is, an anticipation and acceptance of the inevitable sequence of events that will occur as men grow up, grow old, and die—in adulthood, that he understands that the course of his own life will be similar to the lives of others, and that the turning points are inescapable. This ability to interpret the past and foresee the future, and to create for oneself a sense of the predictable life-cycle, differentiates the healthy adult personality from the unhealthy, and it underlies the adult's self-assessment" (1969: 125).

6. Bellah et al. (1985: 71–75) speak of these circles of social intimates formed on the basis of lifestyle as "life-style enclaves." These lifestyle enclaves are segmentary in two senses: they involve only a segment of each individual, for they concern only private life, especially leisure and consumption; and they are segmentary socially in that they include only those with a common lifestyle. See also

Michael J. Weiss (1988) for a study of the overall distribution of the various lifestyle enclaves found throughout the United States.

7. For examples of societies that emphasize the social engagement of self, see Geertz 1973; Devos and Hsu 1985; and Shweder and Bourne 1984. I have to note here, however, that the popular "egocentric versus sociocentric" dichotomy applied commonly to distinguish the Western notion of the self from those of other societies (namely Eastern) has been re-examined in more recent scholarship. McHugh showed that for the Gurungs of Nepal, the high value they place on relationships with others does not preclude a well-defined concept of the individual as a discrete entity with distinct needs and impulses that may run counter to demands for social cohesion (1989); Raybeck finds in traditional, highly stratified Malay society, in which mobility is inhibited and individuals are largely defined in terms of the groups to which they belong, "a goodly degree of individual uniqueness and an emphasis on individual needs" (1989). See also Plath's provocative analysis of Japanese individuals and individuality (1980).

8. Dorothy Lee writes that definitions of the self in American society "rest on our law of contradiction. The self cannot be self and not self, both self and other; the self excludes the other." She then contrasts this with the concept of the self held by the Wintu Indians of Northern California, in which the self "has no strict bounds, is not named, and is not recognized as a separate entity" (1959: 131).

9. Bellah et al. 1985: 81–83.

10. See, for example, Bellah et al. 1985; Veroff, Douvan, and Kulka 1981; and Keyes (1973).

11. This trio of American scholars observed that between the years 1957 and 1976 there were noticeable changes in the coping styles of Americans, including: (1) the diminution of role standards as the basis for defining adjustment; (2) an increased focus on self-expressiveness and self-direction in social life; (3) a shift in concern from social organizational integration to interpersonal intimacy. And the encompassing theme of these three changes was a shift from a socially integrated paradigm for structuring well-being to a more personal or individuated paradigm (1981: 529).

12. Veroff, Douvan, and Kulka 1981, in Bellah et al. 1985: 319.

13. Riesman 1961; Lasch 1979; and Bellah et al. 1985.

14. Plath contrasts the American notion of the self with that of the Japanese. Acknowledging that the Japanese, contrary to popular views held in the West, do treasure individuality and uniqueness, he argues eloquently that there is a qualitative difference in the ways the two societies conceptualize what constitutes individuality: "Our cultural nightmare is that the individual throb of growth will be sucked dry in slavish social conformity. All life long, our central struggle is to defend the individual from the collective. . . . The Japanese cultural nightmare is to be excluded from others, for this renders one unable to do anything with his 'personality.' . . . The American archetype, in short, seems more attuned to cultivating a self that knows it is unique in the cosmos, the Japanese archetype to a self that can feel human in the company of others" (1980: 216–18).

15. Much has been written about the notion of Japanese self since the publication of the work by Plath quoted above (Edwards 1989; Kondo 1990; Rosenberger 1992). However, most of the writings on this subject by American anthropologists in recent years lack a life-course perspective. See Ikeda 1993 for my critique of one such study.

16. See Ishida 1993 for a sociologist's view of social reproduction in Japan.

17. Reported in the *Japan Times*, May 14–20, 1990. The results were based on responses from 1,172 Japanese high school students from fourteen schools and 1,069 American high school students from eleven schools. This article interpreted the findings to mean that Japanese students are "less ambitious" than American students.

18. I must note here, though, that higher dropout rates in American high schools attest to the fact that there are students who lose faith in this ideal at an early age. There is clearly a discrepancy between the cultural ideal and actual practice. In assessing the American education system, most scholars today argue that schools serve to reproduce social structure. For recent examples, see Eckert 1989; Foley 1990; and MacLeod 1987.

19. See essays in the volume on work and the lifecourse in Japan edited by Plath (1983).

20. See also Myerhoff 1979, 1986.
21. "Reunions: A Chance to Gauge Yourself," *News-Gazette*, Aug. 19, 1984.
22. See Myerhoff's analysis (1974) of the peyote hunt of the Huichol Indians for an example. Their ritual return to Wirikuta brings together the 4,000–5,000 dispersed members of the group and links them with the land of their divine ancestors and of their origin.

BIBLIOGRAPHY

Agar, Michael. 1980. "Stories, Background Knowledge, and Themes: Problems in the Analysis of Life History Narrative." *American Ethnologist* 7, no. 2: 223–39.

Babcock, Barbara A. 1980. "Reflexivity: Definitions and Discriminations." *Semiotica* 30, no. 1/2: 1–14.

Barker, Roger G., and Paul V. Gump. 1964. *Big School, Small School: High School Size and Student Behavior.* Stanford, Calif.: Stanford University Press.

Basso, Keith H. 1984. " 'Stalking with Stories': Names, Places, and Moral Narratives Among the Western Apache." In *Text, Play, and Story,* ed. Bruner, pp. 19–55.

Bateson, Gregory. 1972. *Steps to an Ecology of Mind.* New York: Ballantine Books.

Bellah, Robert N., Richard Madsen, William M. Sullivan, Ann Swidler, and Steven M. Tipton. 1985. *Habits of the Heart: Individualism and Commitment in American Life.* New York: Harper and Row.

Berger, Peter L., and Thomas Luckman. 1967. *The Social Construction of Reality.* New York: Anchor Books.

Berger, Peter, Brigitte Berger, and Hansfried Kellner. 1973. *The Home-*

less Mind: Modernization and Consciousness. New York: Vintage Books.

Berman, Marshall. 1987 [1982]. *All That Is Solid Melts into Thin Air.* New York: Penguin Books.

Bersani, Leo. 1976. *A Future for Astyanax: Character and Desire in Literature.* Boston: Little, Brown.

Bestor, Theodore C. 1989. *Neighborhood Tokyo.* Stanford, Calif.: Stanford University Press.

Brown, Ray B. 1985. "Class Reunions as a Folk Festival." *Journal of Popular Culture* 19, no. 1: 107–13.

Bruner, Edward M., ed. 1984. *Text, Play, and Story: The Construction and Reconstruction of Self and Society: 1983 Proceedings of the American Ethnological Society.* Washington, D.C.: American Ethnological Society.

———. 1986. "Experience and Its Expressions." In *The Anthropology of Experience,* ed. Turner and Bruner, pp. 3–30.

———. 1987. "Megaliths, Migration, and the Segmented Self." In *Cultures and Societies of North Sumatra,* ed. Rainer Carle, pp. 133–49. Berlin: Dietrich Reimer Verlag.

Burke, Kenneth. 1945. *A Grammar of Motives.* Englewood Cliffs, N.J.: Prentice-Hall.

———. 1966. *Language as Symbolic Action.* Berkeley: University of California Press.

Butler, Robert N. 1963. "The Life Review: An Interpretation of Reminiscence in the Aged." *Psychiatry* 26, no. 1: 65–76.

Carlinsky, Dan. 1982. *Celebrity Yearbook.* Los Angeles: Prince/Stern/Sloan.

Cather, Willa. 1949 [1918]. *My Antonia.* Cambridge, Mass.: Riverside Press.

Clifford, James. 1986. "On Ethnographic Allegory." In *Writing Culture,* ed. Clifford and Marcus, pp. 98–121.

———. 1988. *The Predicament of Culture: Twentieth-Century Ethnography, Literature, and Art.* Cambridge, Mass.: Harvard University Press.

Clifford, James, and George E. Marcus, eds. 1986. *Writing Culture: The Poetics and Politics of Ethnography.* Berkeley: University of California Press.

Cohen, Anthony P. 1985. *The Symbolic Construction of Community.* New York: Tavistock.

Cohler, Bertram. 1982. "Personal Narrative and Life Course." In *Life-Span Development and Behavior*, vol. 4, ed. Paul Baltes and Orville G. Brim, Jr., pp. 205–29. New York: Academic Press.

Coleman, James S. 1961. *The Adolescent Society*. Glencoe, Ill.: Free Press.

Coleman, James S., et al. 1974. *Youth: Transition to Adulthood*. Chicago: University of Chicago Press.

Coleman, Richard P., and Les Rainwater. 1978. *Social Standing in America: New Dimensions of Class*. New York: Basic Books.

Conant, James B. 1959. *The American High School Today*. New York: McGraw-Hill.

Coser, Rose Laub. 1969. *Life Cycle and Achievement in America*. New York: Harper and Row.

Davis, Fred. 1979. *Yearning for Yesterday: A Sociology of Nostalgia*. New York: Free Press.

Demos, John. 1978. "Old Age in Early New England." In *Turning Points: Historical and Sociological Essays on the Family*, ed. John Demos and Sarane Spence Boocock. Chicago: University of Chicago Press.

Demos, John, and Virginia Demos. 1969. "Adolescence in Historical Perspective." *Journal of Marriage and the Family* 31, no. 4: 632–38.

DeMott, Benjamin. 1992. *The Imperial Middle: Why Americans Can't Think Straight About Class*. New Haven, Conn.: Yale University Press.

Dilthey, Wilhelm. 1961 [1910]. *Pattern and Meaning in History*, ed. H. P. Richman. New York: Harper and Row.

Durkheim, Emile. 1961 [1912]. *The Elementary Forms of Religious Life*. Trans. J. S. Swain. New York: Collier Books.

Eckert, Penelope. 1989. *Jocks and Burnouts: Social Categories and Identity in the High School*. New York: Teachers College Press.

Edwards, Walter. 1989. *Modern Japan Through Its Weddings: Gender, Person, and Society in Ritual Portrayal*. Stanford, Calif.: Stanford University Press.

Erikson, Erik H. 1963 [1950]. *Childhood and Society*. New York: Norton.

——. 1968. *Identity, Youth, and Crisis*. New York: Norton.

——, ed. 1978. *Adulthood*. New York: Norton.

Fernandez, James. 1980. "Reflections on Looking into Mirrors." *Semiotica* 30, no. 1/2: 27–39.

——. 1986. "The Argument of Images and the Experience of Returning to the Whole." In *The Anthropology of Experience*, ed. Turner and Bruner, pp. 159–84.

Fiske, Marjorie. 1980. "Changing Hierarchies of Commitment in Adulthood." In *Themes of Work and Love in Adulthood*, ed. Smelser and Erikson, pp. 238–64.

Foley, D. E. 1990. *Learning Capitalist Culture: Deep in the Heart of Tejas.* Philadelphia: University of Pennsylvania Press.

Fox, Richard G. 1991. *Recapturing Anthropology: Working in the Present.* Santa Fe, N.M.: School of American Research Press.

Frank, Gelya. 1979. "Finding the Common Denominator: A Phenomenological Critique of Life History Method." *Ethos* 7, no. 1: 68–94.

Friedenberg, Edgar Z. 1959. *The Vanishing Adolescent.* Boston: Beacon Press.

———. 1963. *Coming of Age in America: Growth and Acquiescence.* New York: Alfred A. Knopf.

Fussell, Paul. 1983. *Class.* New York: Ballantine Books.

Gadamer, Hans-Georg. 1982. "Text and Interpretation." Paper presented at the Conference on the Philosophy of Human Studies, Philadelphia.

Geertz, Clifford. 1973. *The Interpretation of Culture.* New York: Basic Books.

———. 1983. *Local Knowledge.* New York: Basic Books.

Gennep, Arnold van. 1960 [1909]. *The Rites of Passage.* Trans. Monika B. Vizdom and Gabrielle L. Laffee. Chicago: University of Chicago Press.

Giele, Janet Zollinger. 1980. "Adulthood as Transcendence of Age and Sex." In *Themes of Work and Love in Adulthood*, ed. Smelser and Erikson, pp. 151–73.

Goffman, Erving. 1959. *The Presentation of Self in Everyday Life.* Garden City, N.Y.: Anchor Books.

———. 1974. *Frame Analysis.* New York: Harper Colophon Books.

Goodman, Ellen. 1979. *Turning Points.* New York: Fawcett Columbine.

Gordon, Wayne. 1957. *The Social System of the High School.* Glencoe, Ill.: Free Press.

Gould, Roger L. 1978. *Transformations: Growth and Change in Adult Life.* New York: Simon and Schuster.

Halle, David. 1984. *America's Working Man: Work, Home, and Politics*

Among Blue-Collar Property Owners. Chicago: University of Chicago Press.

Hallowell, Irving A. 1967 [1955]. *Culture and Experience.* New York: Schocken Books.

Hareven, Tamara. 1978. "The Search for Generational Memory: Tribal Rites in Industrial Society." *Daedalus* 107, no. 4: 137–49.

Hebb, Donald 1949. *The Organization of Behavior.* New York: Wiley.

Hill, Jacquetta. 1974 [1969]. "Ceremony, Rites, and Economy in the Student System of an American High School." In *Anthropology and American Life*, ed. Joseph G. Jorgensen and Marcello Truzzi, pp. 290–304. Englewood Cliffs, N.J.: Prentice-Hall.

Hochschild, Arlie Russel. 1978. *The Unexpected Community.* Berkeley: University of California Press.

Humphrey, Lin T., and Theodore C. Humphrey. 1985. "The High School Reunion: A Traditional Festival?" *Journal of Popular Culture* 19, no. 1: 99–106.

Ikeda, Keiko. 1990. "Fighting Festival: The Symbolic Construction of Tradition and Community in Post-Industrial Japan." Paper presented at the annual meeting of the American Anthropological Association, New Orleans.

——. 1993. Review of *Crafting Selves: Power, Gender, and Discourses of Identity in a Japanese Workplace*, by Dorinne K. Kondo, and *Crested Kimono: Power and Love in the Japanese Business Family*, by Matthew Masayuki Hamabata. *American Journal of Sociology* (May): 1475–78.

Inagaki, Tadahiko. 1986. "School Education: Its History and Contemporary Status." In *Child Development and Education in Japan*, ed. Harold Stevenson, Hiroshi Azuma, and Kenji Hakuta, pp. 75–92.

Ishida, Hiroshi. 1993. *Social Mobility in Contemporary Japan: Educational Credentials, Class, and the Labour Market in a Cross National Perspective.* Stanford, Calif.: Stanford University Press.

James, William. 1890. *The Principles of Psychology.* New York: H. Holt and Company.

——. 1892. *Psychology: Briefer Course.* New York: H. Holt and Company.

Japanese Ministry of Education. 1996. *Monbushō tōkei yōran* (Ministry of Education Statistical Handbook).

Jordan, Winthrop D. 1976. "Searching for Adulthood in America." *Daedalus* 105, no. 4: 1–11.

Keniston, Kenneth. 1965. *The Uncommitted: Alienated Youth in American Society*. New York: Harcourt, Brace.

———. 1968. *Young Radicals: Notes on Committed Youth*. New York: Harcourt, Brace.

Kett, Joseph F. 1977. *Rites of Passage: Adolescence in America, 1790 to the Present*. New York: Basic Books.

Keyes, Ralph. 1973. *We, the Lonely People*. New York: Harper and Row.

———. 1976. *Is There Life After High School?* Boston: Little, Brown.

Kiefer, Chris. 1974. "The Psychological Interdependence of Family, School, and Bureaucracy in Japan." In *Japanese Culture and Behavior*, ed. Takie Sugiyama Lebra and William P. Lebra, pp. 342–56. Honolulu: University of Hawaii Press.

Kirschner, Suzanne R. 1987. " 'Then What Have I to Do with Thee?': On Identity, Fieldwork, and Ethnographic Knowledge." *Cultural Anthropology* 2, no. 2: 211–34.

Kluckhohn, Clyde. 1945. "The Personal Document in Anthropological Science." In *The Use of Personal Documents in History, Anthropology, and Sociology*, ed. Louis Gottschalk, Clyde Kluckhohn, and Robert Angell, pp. 79–103. New York: Social Science Research Council Bulletin no. 53.

Kondo, Dorinne. 1990. *Crafting Selves: Power, Gender, and Discourse of Identity in a Japanese Workplace*. Chicago: University of Chicago Press.

Lakoff, George, and Mark Johnson. 1980. *Metaphors We Live By*. Chicago: University of Chicago Press.

Lamb, Douglas H., and Glenn D. Reeder. 1986. "Reliving Golden Days." *Psychology Today* (June): 22–30.

Langness, L. L., and Gelya Frank. 1981. *Lives: An Anthropological Approach to Biography*. Novato, Calif.: Chandler and Sharp.

Lasch, Christopher. 1979. *The Culture of Narcissism*. New York: Norton.

Lebra, Takie Sugiyama. 1982 [1976]. *Japanese Patterns of Behavior*. Honolulu: University of Hawaii Press.

Lee, Dorothy. 1959. *Freedom and Culture*. Englewood Cliffs, N.J.: Prentice-Hall.

LeVine, Robert A. 1980. "Adulthood Among the Gusii of Kenya." In *Themes of Work and Love in Adulthood,* ed. Smelser and Erikson, pp. 77–104.

Levinson, Daniel. 1980. "Toward a Conception of the Adult Life Course." In *Themes of Work and Love in Adulthood,* ed. Smelser and Erikson, pp. 265–90.

Lifton, Robert Jay. 1971. "Protean Man." In *History and Human Survival,* pp. 311–31. New York: Random House.

Linde, C. 1987. "Explanatory Systems in Oral Life Stories." In *Cultural Models in Language and Thought,* ed. Dorothy Holland and Naomi Quinn, pp. 343–66. New York: Cambridge University Press.

Lynd, Robert S., and Helen Merrell Lynd. 1956 [1929]. *Middletown: A Study in Modern American Culture.* New York: Harcourt, Brace.

MacLeod, J. 1987. *Ain't No Makin' It.* Boulder, Colo.: Westview Press.

Malanowski, Jamie, Susan Morrison, and the Editors of *Spy.* 1991. *A Make-Believe Yearbook of America's Rich and Famous.* New York: Dolphin Books.

Marcus, George E., and Michael M. J. Fischer. 1986. *Anthropology as Cultural Critique: An Experimental Movement in the Human Sciences.* Chicago: University of Chicago Press.

Markey, Judy. 1984. *How to Survive Your High School Reunion . . . and Other Midlife Crises.* Chicago: Contemporary Books.

Marsella, Anthony J., George Devos, and Francis L. K. Hsu, eds. 1985. *Culture and Self: Asian and Western Perspectives.* New York: Tavistock.

Matthews, Sarah H. 1986. *Friendships Through the Life Course.* Beverly Hills, Calif.: Sage.

Mauss, Marcel. 1938. "Une catégorie de l'esprit humain: la notion de personne celle de 'moi': un plan de travail." *Journal of the Royal Anthropological Institute* 68: 63–281.

McHugh, Ernestine L. 1989. "Concepts of the Person Among the Gurungs of Nepal." *American Ethnologist* 16, no. 1: 75–86.

Mead, George Herbert. 1932. *The Philosophy of the Present.* La Salle, Ill.: Open Court.

——. 1962 [1934]. *Mind, Self, and Society.* Chicago: University of Chicago Press.

Mead, Robert Douglas. 1973. *Reunion.* New York: Saturday Review Press.

Merelman, Richard M. 1984. *Making Something of Ourselves: On Culture and Politics in the United States*. Berkeley: University of California Press.

Miller, Arthur. 1949. *Death of a Salesman*. New York: Colonial Press.

Miller, David L. 1973. *George Herbert Mead: Self, Language, and the World*. Chicago: University of Chicago Press.

———. 1982. *The Individual and the Social Self*. Chicago: University of Chicago Press.

Moffatt, Michael. 1992. "Ethnographic Writing About American Culture." *Annual Review of Anthropology* 21: 205–29.

Myerhoff, Barbara. 1974. *Peyote Hunt: The Sacred Journey of the Huichol Indians*. Ithaca, N.Y.: Cornell University Press.

———. 1977. "We Don't Wrap Herring in a Printed Page: Fusions, Fictions, and Continuity in Secular Ritual." In *Secular Ritual*, ed. Myerhoff and Moore, pp. 199–224.

———. 1978. *Number Our Days*. New York: Simon and Schuster.

———. 1980. "Re-membered Lives." *Parabola* 5, no. 1: 74–77.

———. 1984. "Rites and Signs of Ripening: The Intertwining of Ritual, Time, and Growing Older." In *Age and Anthropological Theory*, ed. David I. Kertzer and Jennie Keith, pp. 305–30. Ithaca, N.Y.: Cornell University Press.

Myerhoff, Barbara, and Deena Metzger. 1980. "The Journal as Activity and Genre; Or, Listening to the Silent Laughter of Mozart." *Semiotica* 30, no. 1/2: 97–114.

Myerhoff, Barbara, and Sally F. Moore, eds. 1977. *Secular Ritual*. Assen and Amsterdam: Van Gorcum.

National Center for Education Statistics. 1987. *Digest of Education Statistics*. Washington, D.C.: U.S. Department of Health, Education, and Welfare.

National Lampoon. 1974. *1964 High School Yearbook Parody*. New York: National Lampoon.

Neugarten, Bernice L. 1969. "Continuities and Discontinuities of Psychological Issues into Adult Life." *Human Development* 12: 121–30.

———, ed. 1968. *Middle Age and Aging*. Chicago: University of Chicago Press.

Neugarten, Bernice L., and Nancy Datan. 1973. "Sociological Perspective on the Life Cycle." In *Life-Span Developmental Psychology:*

Personality and Socialization, ed. P. Baltes and K. Schaic. New York: Academic Press.

Odendahl, Teresa. 1990. *Charity Begins at Home: Generosity and Self-Interest Among the Philanthropic Elite*. New York: Basic Books.

Olney, James. 1980. "Biography, Autobiography and the Life Course." In *Life Course: Integrative Theories and Exemplary Populations*, ed. Kurt W. Back, pp 27–36. Boulder, Colo.: Westview Press.

Ortner, Sherry. 1973. "On Key Symbols." *American Anthropologist* 75, no. 5: 1338–46.

———. 1991. "Reading America: Preliminary Notes on Class and Culture." In *Recapturing Anthropology: Working in the Present*, ed. Fox, pp 163–89.

Östör, Ákos. 1984. "Chronology, Category, and Ritual" In *Age and Anthropological Theory*, ed. David I. Kertzer and Jennie Keith, pp. 280–304. Ithaca, N.Y.: Cornell University Press.

Paris, Scott G., and Barbara K. Lindauer. 1977. "Constructive Aspects of Children's Comprehension and Memory." In *Perspectives on the Development of Memory and Cognition*, ed. R. V. Kail, Jr., and J. W. Hagen. Hillsdale, N.J.: Erlbaum.

Parsons, Talcott. 1959. "The School Class as a Social System: Some of Its Functions in American Society." *Harvard Educational Review* 29, no. 4: 297–318.

Paul, Irving H. 1959. *Studies in Remembering: The Reproduction of Connected and Extended Verbal Material*. Psychological Issues, vol. 1. New York: International Universities Press.

———. 1967. "The Concept of Schema in Memory Theory." In *Motives and Thoughts: Psychoanalytic Essays in Honor of David Rapaport*, ed. Robert R. Holt, pp. 218–58. Psychological Issues, vol. 5. New York: International Universities Press.

Peacock, James. 1984. "Religion and Life History: An Exploration in Cultural Psychology." In *Text, Play, and Story*, ed. Bruner, pp. 94–115.

Pearlin, Leonard I. 1980. "Life Strains and Psychological Distress among Adults." In *Themes of Work and Love in Adulthood*, ed. Smelser and Erikson, pp. 174–92.

Plath, David W. 1980. *Long Engagements: Maturity in Modern Japan*. Stanford, Calif.: Stanford University Press.

———, ed. 1983. *Work and Lifecourse in Japan*. Albany: State University of New York Press.

Plath, David W., and Keiko Ikeda. 1975. "After Coming of Age: Adult Awareness of Age Norms." In *Socialization and Communication in Primary Groups*, ed. Thomas R. Williams, pp. 107–23. The Hague: Mouton, and Chicago: Aldine.

Rabinow, Paul, and William M. Sullivan, eds. 1979. *Interpretive Social Science: A Reader*. Berkeley: University of California Press.

Rappaport, Roy A. 1980. "Concluding Comments on Ritual and Reflexivity." *Semiotica* 30, no. 1/2: 181–93.

Raybeck, Douglas. 1989. "I and Thou, Us and Them: Individual and the Group in Peasant Society." Paper presented at the annual meeting of the American Anthropological Association, Washington, D.C.

Reck, Andrew J. 1964. *Selected Writings of George Herbert Mead*. Chicago: University of Chicago Press.

Reese, William J. 1995. *The Origins of the American High School*. New Haven, Conn.: Yale University Press.

Reinhardt, Emme. 1966. "Development of Secondary Education." In *Secondary Education*, ed. Lawrence E. Metcalf et al., pp. 11–19. Boston: Allyn and Bacon.

Ricoeur, Paul. 1970. *Freud and Philosophy*. New Haven, Conn.: Yale University Press.

———. 1977. "Proof in Freud's Psychoanalytic Writings." *Journal of the American Psychoanalytic Association* 25: 835–72.

———. 1979 [1971]. "The Model of Text: Meaningful Action Considered as a Text." In *Interpretive Social Science*, ed. Rabinow and Sullivan, pp. 73–101.

Riegel, Klaus F. 1977. "The Dialectics of Time." In *Life-Span Developmental Psychology: Dialectic Perspectives on Experimental Research*, ed. Nancy Datan and Howard Reeve, pp. 3–45. New York: Academic Press.

Riesman, David. 1961 [1950]. *The Lonely Crowd*. New Haven, Conn.: Yale University Press.

Rohlen, Thomas. 1983. *Japan's High Schools*. Berkeley: University of California Press.

Rosaldo, Michelle Z. 1980. *Knowledge and Passion: Ilongot Notions of Self and Social Life*. New York: Cambridge University Press.

———. 1984. "Toward an Anthropology of Self and Feeling." In *Culture Theory*, ed. Shweder and LeVine, pp. 137–57.

Rosaldo, Renato. 1976. "The Story of Tukbaw: 'They Listen as He Orates.'" In *The Biographical Process: Studies in the History and Psychology of Religion*, ed. Frank E. Reynolds and Donald Copp, pp. 121–51. The Hague: Mouton.

———. 1984. "Grief and the Headhunter's Rage: On the Cultural Forces of Emotions." In *Text, Play, and Story*, ed. Bruner, pp. 178–95.

———. 1986. "Ilongot Hunting as Story and Experience." In *The Anthropology of Experience*, ed. Turner and Bruner, pp. 97–138.

———. 1989. *Culture and Truth: The Remaking of Social Analysis*. Boston: Beacon Press.

Rosenberger, Nancy. 1992. *Japanese Sense of Self*. New York: Cambridge University Press.

Rosenwald, George C., and Richard L. Ochberg. 1992. *Storied Lives: The Cultural Politics of Self-Understanding*. New Haven, Conn.: Yale University Press.

Roth, Julius A. 1963. *Timetables: Structuring the Passage of Time in Hospital Treatment and Other Careers*. Indianapolis, Ind.: Bobbs-Merrill.

Saint-Exupéry, Antoine de. 1939. *Wind, Sand, and Stars*. Trans. Lewis Galantière. New York: Reynal and Hitchock.

Sameroff, Arnold J., and Michael J. Chandler. 1975. "Reproductive Risk and the Continuum of Caretaking Casualty." In *Review of Child Development Research*, vol. 4, ed. Frances D. Horowitz, pp. 187–244. Chicago: University of Chicago Press.

Sanjek, Roger, ed. 1990. *Fieldnotes: Makings of Anthropology*. Ithaca, N.Y.: Cornell University Press.

Sapir, Edward. 1956 [1949]. *Culture, Language, and Personality*. Ed. David G. Mandelbaum. Berkeley: University of California Press.

Sapir, J. David, and J. Christopher Crocker, eds. 1977. *The Social Use of Metaphors: Essays on the Anthropology of Rhetoric*. Philadelphia: University of Pennsylvania Press.

Scheff, T. J. 1979. *Catharsis in Healing, Ritual, and Drama*. Berkeley: University of California Press.

Schieffelin, Edward L. 1976. *The Sorrow of the Lonely and the Burning of the Dancers*. New York: St. Martin's Press.

Schneider, David M., and Raymond T. Smith. 1973. *Class Differences and*

Sex Roles in American Kinship and Family Structure. Englewood Cliffs, N.J.: Prentice-Hall.

Schutz, Alfred. 1945. "The Homecomer." *American Journal of Sociology* 50, no. 5: 367–76.

———. 1970. *On Phenomenology and Social Relations.* Ed. R. Wagner. Chicago: University of Chicago Press.

Schwarts, Garry, and Don Merten. 1967. "The Language of Adolescence: An Anthropological Approach to the Youth Culture." *American Journal of Sociology* 72, no. 5: 453–68.

Sheehy, Gail. 1977. *Passages: Predictable Crises of Adult Life.* New York: Bantam Books.

Shweder, Richard A., and Robert LeVine. 1984. "Does the Concept of the Person Vary Cross-Culturally?" In *Culture Theory,* ed. Shweder and LeVine, pp. 158–99.

———, eds. 1984. *Culture Theory: Essays on Mind, Self, and Emotion.* New York: Cambridge University Press.

Smelser, Neil J., and Erik H. Erikson, eds. 1980. *Themes of Work and Love in Adulthood.* Cambridge, Mass.: Harvard University Press.

Smelser, Neil. 1980. "Issues in the Study of Work and Love in Adulthood." In *Themes of Work and Love in Adulthood,* ed. Smelser and Erikson, pp. 1–26.

Swenson, Greta. 1989. *Festivals of Sharing: Family Reunions in America.* New York: AMS Press.

Swidler, Ann. 1980. "Love and Adulthood in American Culture." In *Themes of Work and Love in Adulthood,* ed. Smelser and Erikson, pp. 120–47.

Tilton, Jeff. 1980. "The Life Story." *Journal of American Folklore* 93, no. 367: 276–92.

Tocqueville, Alexis de. 1945. *Democracy in America.* Ed. Phillips Bradley. New York: Vintage Books.

Turner, Victor W. 1974. *Drama, Fields, and Metaphors.* Ithaca, N.Y.: Cornell University Press.

———. 1977. *The Ritual Process.* Ithaca, N.Y.: Cornell University Press.

Turner, Victor W., and Edward M. Bruner, eds. 1986. *The Anthropology of Experience.* Urbana: University of Illinois Press.

U.S. Department of Education. 1987. *Japanese Education Today.* Washington, D.C.: U.S. Department of Education.

Valliant, George. 1977. *Adaptation to Life.* Boston: Little, Brown.

Veroff, Joseph, Elizabeth Douvan, and Richard A. Kulka. 1981. *The Inner American: A Self-Portrait from 1957 to 1976.* New York: Basic Books.

Vonnegut, Kurt, Jr. 1970. "Times Change: Reflections of a High School Student from the Class of '40." *Esquire* (Feb.): 60–63.

Watson, Lawrence C. 1976. "Understanding of a Life History as a Subjective Document: Hermeneutical and Phenomenological Perspectives." *Ethos* 4, no. 1: 95–131.

Watson, Lawrence C., and Maria-Barbara Watson-Franke. 1985. *Interpreting Life Histories: An Anthropological Inquiry.* New Brunswick, N.J.: Rutgers University Press.

Weiss, Michael J. 1988. *Clustering of America.* New York: Harper and Row.

White, Merry. 1993. *The Material Child: Coming of Age in Japan and America.* New York: Free Press.

White, Robert. 1966. *Lives in Progress.* New York: Holt, Rinehart.

Wolf, Margery. 1992. *A Thrice-Told Tale: Feminism, Postmodernism, and Ethnographic Responsibility.* Stanford, Calif.: Stanford University Press.

INDEX

In this index an "f" after a number indicates a separate reference on the next page, and an "ff" indicates separate references on the next two pages. A continuous discussion over two or more pages is indicated by a span of page numbers. *Passim* is used for a cluster of references in close but not consecutive sequence.

Library of Congress Cataloguing-in-Publication Data

Ikeda, Keiko.
A room full of mirrors : high school reunions in middle America /
Keiko Ikeda.
    p. cm.
Includes bibliographical references (p.   ) and index.
ISBN 0-8047-3435-6 (alk. paper)
1. Class reunions—United States.   2. High schools—United
States.   I. Title.
LB3618.I54   1998
371.8′9—dc21   98-7111

⊗ This book is printed on acid-free, recycled paper.

Original printing 1998
Last figure below indicates year of this printing:
07   06   05   04   03   02   01   00   99   98